An Inconvenient Life

My Unconventional Career as a Wellsite
Geologist

By Amanda Barlow

Cover: Alex Dumitru – Image Trance
imagetrance@gmail.com

ISBN: 978-1-530-93934-3

DISCLAIMER

This book depicts the author's own experiences as a geologist. As the subtitle of the book suggests, the author's career path was unconventional and it is by no means a blueprint for aspiring geologists to follow, but rather to show how being resourceful and proactive in an industry famous for its cyclical booms and busts is necessary if you are to survive and remain employed in the industry.

This book is dedicated to all the fly-in, fly-out workers in the resources sector who have made the choice to spend several months of the year working in remote locations around the world, away from family and friends, a way of life. The "upstream" operations are where it all starts – if there were no people to sacrifice their time living out in the exploration camps then there would be no resource industry. Not only do we sacrifice a lot to be at our jobs but we are always the first to be slashed when there is a downturn – and when you're a contractor there's no pay-out, quite often no thank-you, just the knowing that you no longer have a job at the end of this hitch. You forever live from one hitch to the next not knowing if it will be your last. It's only when you can be more excited about your unpredictable job than scared stiff of its unpredictability that you know you're in the right place.

CONTENTS

ACKNOWLEDGMENTS

This book was born from an idea given to me by friend Natalie Taylor while I was discussing the severe job losses in the offshore drilling industry. After expressing my concern she said: "well, why don't you write about it?"...So I did!

Special thanks to the following people for helping me remember the pieces of the puzzle that I was missing from the Rockdril days: Gary Barlow, Bain Webster, Iain Blaney, Shane Hibbird, Gordon Wakelin-King.

Also, thanks to the following people who helped me track down 30-year-old historical well data: Bernadette McCormack and David Murchie from the Geological Survey of Queensland, Bronwyn Witham from the Geoscience Databases Geological Survey of NSW and Nicky McMaster from the Northern Territory Government Department of Mines and Energy. Your time and guidance to navigate the government databases was invaluable and every time I found exactly the report I was looking for I would be punching the air in excitement! The Well Completion Reports were always compiled and submitted to the Government long after our drilling rig had left the well location so going back and reading the official reports of wells we not only "worked on" but literally "lived on" actually made me feel a sense of pride in being involved in the projects. Seeing the names on the reports of people who were on the jobs brought back great memories, not just of a drill hole but of all the fun we had in the drilling camps and on road trips between the wells.

A very special thanks to my amazing cover designer,

Alex Dumitru of Image Trance, who never fails to capture the essence of who I am and the message I'm trying to get across in the cover of my book, despite never having met me face-to-face. Our lengthy Messenger conversations while designing the cover were so much fun and despite living on opposite sides of the world you still managed to deliver the goods in record time. Your dedication to getting it absolutely right is a credit to you and your professionalism.

And finally a huge thank-you to ex-geologist, now awesome photographer (www.buddphotography.com.au) and long time best friend, Roslyn Budd, for proof-reading and editing my manuscript. If anyone knows my life story it's Ros, so she was the obvious choice for proofreading it before setting it free on the public. You're still a geo in my eyes Ros!

INTRODUCTION

I can remember in Grade 4 doing a project on the Geological Time Scale and already knowing that I wanted to be a geologist. I would have had no idea back then what a geologist actually does for a living but all I knew was that I was fascinated by the earth and the rocks that covered it. Nearly 50 years later I still love the hands-on geology and that's why I prefer to be working "in the field" rather than in an office in town looking at drill hole results on paper reports instead of real rocks. Being the first person to see the drilled samples in a multi-million dollar drilling campaign still gets me excited even after 30 years of working around drilling rigs. From the spectacular massive sulphide samples in remote minesites to the fossilized remains of sea creatures and hydrocarbon deposits buried under kilometres of sediments that can also lie beneath kilometres of water in deep offshore basins, I've remained hooked. Every drill hole is different and whether it ends up being an economic discovery or not, the samples recovered are still a treasure trove of information about a period in Earth's history millions of years in the past.

Most of my career has been spent working in remote locations that require you to be away from home for weeks, or even months, at a time. Life as a "Fly In – Fly Out" (FIFO) worker in remote areas of the world can be a lonely and inconvenient life if you let it be. Long periods of time spent away from family and friends and quite often not knowing where you'll be from one week to the next, can put a lot of strain on relationships and be far removed from the "normal" life of working 9 to 5 for five days a week. It may be hard to imagine but some people actually not only *enjoy* working FIFO – but *thrive* on it. I'm one of those people.

My family is a FIFO family through and through. My husband of 20 years (but now my ex-husband) has worked FIFO in the minerals sector most of his adult life – 36 years. I have worked FIFO for most of the past 18 years (after being a stay-at-home mum for several years) and our eldest son has been working FIFO in the minerals sector since he was 17 years old, which now has him seeing 12 years in the industry.

I started working FIFO in the Australian minerals industry when my youngest of three children started school. My husband at the time was on a rare couple of years working on a job where he was home every night so it was his turn to look after the kids for a change. As you can guess, I found I had two weeks worth of cleaning and washing to catch up on when I got home after each hitch away and I spent the five days I was at home pre-cooking meals for the freezer and forward planning the kids school activities, so my time at work soon turned into my holiday time. I learned to love my travel days where I didn't have to be a mother, wife or housekeeper nor did I have to be a Geologist. For one day every fortnight it was pure "me" time. The Qantas Lounge became my health spa, an escape from reality. I could relax and read magazines, watch TV without interruptions and eat food that I didn't have to prepare, cook or clean up after.

For many years before that my husband worked a 12-weeks on, 2-weeks off roster working on drilling rigs in the deserts of WA and the Northern Territory (which was standard for the industry in the 1980's before the phrase "Fly-In, Fly-Out was even coined). When I first started working FIFO I was on a 2-weeks on, 1-week off roster but I also had a day of travel each side of that which meant I only had five days at home every three weeks.

My time on that first FIFO contract lasted for an incredible 4 ½ years at a North Queensland minesite and I loved it. After being a stay-at-home-mum for several years I was finally being recognized (and paid!) for my intellectual knowledge and dedication to the job. The mental stimulation of the job and the financial reward on payday were drivers that would be a constant motivational force in my life from then on.

So, what about the kids? Well of course as any mother will tell you, nothing detracts from your maternal instincts. I would ring the kids every night and keep tabs on what they were doing and what happened each day at school. Our lives soon settled into a new "normal" for our family.

After a couple of years of this my husband started working FIFO again so it became a bit more difficult to continue the 2/1 roster I was on. I was able to negotiate a change to a 2-week on, 2-week off roster and for the periods when both me and my husband were away at work we would pay a friend to live in our home and look after the kids. It was a much more manageable roster for me to maintain and I now had lots of time at home with the kids. I had all day, every day, for two weeks at a time to spend with the kids. I purposely never got involved with extra-curricula activities so my time was totally free for the kids when I was home. Of course there is no doubt the kids would have preferred it if I was home all the time but guess what – they don't need your full attention for 24 hours a day, 7 days a week. There are plenty of kids whose parents live at home all the time but they are disadvantaged in some way. The love you show them whether you are in the same room or not is what matters – not having permanent face-to-face time. They were well looked after in my absence so everyone's needs were met. Kids are adaptable. Life shouldn't be rigid.

Of course my lifestyle wasn't without its critics. Many people assume that if you aren't home with your kids then you're a bad mother. Judgmental people are only a problem if you let them be – I didn't.

The main benefit of being a total FIFO family is that our home was never associated with work. There were never the crazy weekday morning stresses of getting kids off to school and getting to work on time only to have to go through the whole stressful process again for the afternoon pick-up and battling traffic to get home then have to prepare dinner, do homework, dishes, washing, and prepare for the next day before trying to get to bed early enough to be able to get up and do it all again the next day. Kids in day care early in the morning till late in the afternoon, road rage in the crazy city traffic, feeling like you're on a crazy treadmill day in, day out. Life wasn't like that for us. We didn't have to get to work each morning so it was only the kids that mattered each day. And now that the kids are all grown up and looking after themselves, my home is like a holiday home; there is no routine or racing around on breaks, it's like going home to my own retreat where my time is my own. No battling traffic each morning, just chilling out and enjoying the fruits of my labour.

For the past 17 years I have worked a mainly even-time roster, which means I have as much time at home as I do at work. Two weeks on, two weeks off or up to four weeks on, four weeks off. For me, a 56-year-old mother of three adult children, it's like a holiday camp. Now working in the offshore oil and gas industry, I have three cooked buffet meals a day, fridges full of desserts, bowls of fruit, soft drink and ice cream available for the taking. There's no cooking or dishes to wash up. When I go back to my room the bed has been made and the room and ensuite bathroom cleaned. Before I go to bed I place my dirty work clothes from that day in a laundry bag on the floor outside my door and when I wake up in the morning the same clothes are washed, folded and placed back in front of my door ready to wear again. No cooking, cleaning or laundry...EVER!! No having to worry about what I'm going to cook for tea when I get home from work – most mothers can only ever dream about that!

And to top it off I'm helping make decisions that will hopefully contribute to the successful drilling of a well that could cost over one hundred million dollars in some cases. And if you are on a successful well then you get the added bonus of seeing a stock market press release announcing the results of a drilling program that can ultimately influence the company's share price. Seeing the share price of the company you have been working for jump after announcing the successful results of a well you have been involved in drilling is a fantastic feeling. It's like the icing on the cake.

****

I'm seventeen years into my FIFO journey now and couldn't have a more harmonious family. I love my life as a single, financially independent female. My ex-husband is my best friend and we have a mutual respect and admiration for each other's careers. The kids are all independent, well-travelled, well-adjusted and adventurous young adults who know that life is only limited by your own imagination. They know that if you don't like the job you are in then you change it. If you can't find your dream job where you live then you move. I'm proud of them and they are proud of me. We recognize that our family is not the "norm" but none of us would want it any other way. We all know that "being stuck in a rut" is never going to apply to us because as soon as we start to think that then we know it's time for another change.

"Change" is exciting, not something to be feared. Being scared stiff and excited all at the same time is what makes "change" so addictive. Putting yourself on the line and knowing you have to either sink or swim is what gives you the courage to take that leap of faith and go after your dreams. Challenging the conventional workforce structure is our way of breaking free from the treadmill of traditional jobs.

The journey to where I am today has been a long and unpredictable one. My 17 years as a contract geologist after returning to the workforce after starting a family, has meant I've had to continually adapt to new projects, work environments and people. As a contractor, your career depends on your professional reputation so you have to make sure you're always striving to add value to the project you're being paid to work on.

This book will outline the unconventional path I have taken to get my career to where it is today. To most people it probably seems that I've had a lot of luck getting the jobs I've had but that couldn't be further from the truth. I've always been proactive and resourceful in making sure I achieved my career goals and then made the most of the opportunities once I'd got to where I wanted to be. My career is never static and I'm continually learning and growing in my chosen field. Growing through the boom times and surviving through the busts is the challenge facing contractors like myself every day. Flexibility, adaptability and resourcefulness are the key traits essential to succeeding.

After beginning my career in the goldfields of Victoria and later in the base metals mineral province of northwest Queensland, I made a choice to try something different and pursued work as a mudlogger in the offshore oil and gas industry. After a few years of this I then returned to onshore mineral drilling programs, then onto wellsite geology work in coal seam gas, followed by a few more years working in base metals near-mine exploration drilling and eventually back offshore into oil and gas as a Wellsite Geologist. Reinventing myself every few years by taking advantage of opportunities when they arose had me continually stepping out of my comfort zone and rising to the challenge of advancing my career in exciting new directions. Continuing education and attending courses is a constant driver that helps me cope with the challenges I set for myself and make sure I give myself the best possible chance of surviving the transition.

I'm now in a role that I'm happy to stay in for the rest of my career. Working offshore can be very challenging and demanding but it's also very rewarding, interesting and exciting. The comraderie amongst the tight-knitted offshore industry helps with the constant transition from home life to work life and the crews on a rig can make or break your hitch at work. While the work is very serious there's always room for a little fun while you're doing it. With 100 to 200 people all living and working in the confines of the rig it's important to get along with everyone because there's going to be 100 to 200 different personalities amongst dozens of different nationalities and cultures. Very few women work offshore and it's not uncommon to be the only female onboard a rig in a workforce of hundreds of men. You just have to accept that there will be times when you surprise naked men opening their bedroom doors to get their laundry out of the corridor, or even having men accidentally enter your room when you're stepping out of the shower totally naked. A good sense of humor is definitely needed then!

My hope is that this book sheds some light on what it's like to work in the resources sector as a field-based geologist, and the challenges facing anyone wanting to make it their career. You definitely have to be prepared to take the bad with the good because it's not all roses out there – far from it. A thick skin and flexible life are bare minimum pre-requisites.

Chapter 1

1983

MY FIRST JOB AS A GEOLOGIST

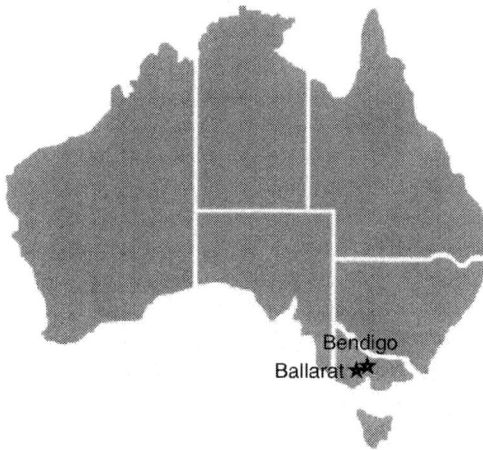

In 1983 I graduated from the Ballarat College of Advanced Education, which was formally known as the School Of Mines Ballarat (SMB), and later became the Ballarat University and is now the Federation University Australia. The Ballarat School of Mines was established in 1871 and was built after the Ballarat Mining Board recognized that there was a shortage of mine managers to service the goldfields. It's the oldest site of technical education in Australia.

Ballarat was one of the pioneer goldfield regions in Australia after rich alluvial gold deposits were discovered there in 1851. Within months, approximately 20,000 migrants had rushed to the district. Unlike many other gold rush boomtowns, the Ballarat fields experienced sustained high gold yields for decades.

While there were no operating mines in the region by the time I started my studies in Ballarat, there was still a lot of interest from small mining companies who were hoping to discover extensions of the gold-rich "Deep Leads."

"Leads" are mineral deposits that are formed by mechanical concentration in the bed of a stream by water action. "Deep Leads" are leads that have been buried by younger rocks (sediment or lava) and the course of the lead cannot be determined by the present topography. The Ballarat "deep leads" are the channel deposits of a widespread middle Cenozoic dendritic drainage system that's now largely buried by basalt. The unit is richly gold bearing because it contains gold derived from bedrock and gold that was reworked and concentrated from gravel deposits.

The Ballarat goldfields are hosted in the kilometres-thick Lower Ordovician Castlemaine Group greenschist grade sequence of quartz-rich turbidites. These rocks were deformed in the Silurian and then intruded in the Devonian by numerous post-tectonic granites. Layers of Cenozoic gravel deposits, that are often rich in placer gold, patchily overlie the bedrock. Cenozoic flood basalts cover much of the region.

****

With Ballarat having such a strong history of gold mining it was to be expected that the geology degree undertaken there would be heavily biased towards gold and base metal geology, with a strong focus on the Victorian goldfields.

Australia was still experiencing growth in minerals exploration, and exporting of our resources was now the country's biggest earner. At the time of my graduation, the biggest resource companies in Australia were:

- **BHP** - Broken Hill Proprietary Company Limited, incorporated in 1885, later merged with the Anglo-Dutch Billiton Plc. in 2001 to become **BHP Billiton**, Australia's largest company and the world's largest mining company.
- **MIM** – Mount Isa Mines Limited, founded in 1924, operated the Mount Isa copper, lead, zinc and silver mines near Mount Isa, Queensland. For a brief period in 1980, MIM was Australia's largest company and it pioneered several significant mining industry innovations. In 2003 the company was taken over by Xstrata and in May 2013, Xstrata merged with Glencore to form Glencore Xstrata Plc. In May 2014, Glencore Xstrata changed its name to Glencore Plc.
- **CRA** - Conzinc Riotinto of Australia was formed in 1962 after the merger of the Spanish company Rio Tinto (which was named after the Rio Tinto River in southwestern Spain, which has flowed red since mining began there about 5000 years ago) and the Australian firm Consolidated Zinc. In 1995 a further company restructuring saw CRA become Rio Tinto Limited.
- **WMC** – Western Mining Corporation was originally founded in 1933 and operated in the

3

goldfields of Western Australia. They were also the original operators of the Olympic Dam Copper-Gold-Uranium mine in South Australia before a successful takeover by BHP Billiton in 2005.

All minesites at this time had a workforce that lived either in existing townships close to the mine or in company towns that were established close to the operations. The three biggest mining towns at the time were Kalgoorlie in Western Australia, Mount Isa in Queensland, and Broken Hill in New South Wales, all of which grew into large cities that serviced the wider rural areas in those states.

Exploration activities were conducted with stand-alone mobile camps where drilling crews and exploration geologists lived for weeks – even months – at a time while drilling programs were conducted.

****

On completion of my Bachelor of Science degree (Geology) at the end of 1983 I secured a position as a Project Geologist with Western Mining Corporation (WMC) in their Bendigo exploration office in the heart of the central Victorian goldfields. My commencement date was the 28th November 1983 and my annual salary was to be $17,000.

With my home base being in Melbourne, I had to relocate to Bendigo, with the company paying for me to stay in a hotel for a couple of weeks while I found more permanent accommodation.

Bendigo is a regional city in the state of Victoria and is

approximately 150 km (93 mi) north west of Melbourne. The population in 1983 was about 60,000 and growing each year. The WMC exploration office was located in the suburb of Eaglehawk and I managed to find accommodation close to the office.

Once I got settled into my new life as a Geologist I decided to join a local gym. I'd never been a sporty person during school but when I was at University I started jogging around the campus roads and even made use of the free entry for university students at the local YMCA pool and taught myself to swim properly. I soon found a keen interest in the fitness industry once I started doing weight training and it was around this time that exercise-to-music classes started to take off. This was the start of what would soon be known as "Aerobics" classes and the beginnings of the fledgling fitness boom that would see gyms as being the "singles bars of the 80's." The classes were a lot of fun and within a few months I found myself working at the gym part-time as a gym instructor and aerobics class instructor. Every day after work I'd head to the gym and either work as an instructor or do my own training. It was a fun environment and I started making a close network of friends in my adoptive city.

****

The geology of the area was very familiar to me as Bendigo lies within the Bendigo-Ballarat zone of the Palaeozoic Lachlan Fold Belt of eastern Australia, which was a heavy focus of our geology degree. The Bendigo

Goldfield is the largest "slate belt" goldfield in the world.

The generalised structure of the Lower Ordovician sediments within the Bendigo Goldfield is that of regular, close spaced folding with extensive local reverse faulting related to the compression event generating the folding. The main characteristics of folds at Bendigo are their regular frequency, continuity along strike, and their strong structural control of gold-quartz mineralisation. The gold mineralisation occurs as free gold in quartz, in association with sulphides in quartz, in association with fragments or laminae of wall rock in quartz and also associated with sulphides in wall rock adjacent to quartz veins.

Surrounding the mineralised quartz reefs is a broad halo of weak hydrothermal alteration consisting of sericite, chlorite, and carbonate and disseminated pyrite. Weak pervasive silicification is also present but is restricted to sandstones.

The intensity of alteration increases as the mineralised quartz reef is approached and large crystals of arsenopyrite are commonly present within a few metres of the mineralised reef. Typical "Bendigo style" reefs occur in close proximity to the anticline axes. Conventional saddle reefs occupy the dilational void of the fold hinge. These are usually small in sectional area but extensive along strike.

The exploration drilling programs undertaken by WMC were diamond coring drillholes and reverse circulation (RC) drilling which were targeting the saddle reefs in the anticlinal fold hinges. My job entailed supervising the drill rigs and also logging the diamond core and RC samples. Bedding plane and cleavage angles were measured in the core as well as recording all mineralisation, lithology and structural details. As the gold was always associated with quartz veining it was always exciting when the drillers intersected quartz veins, as there was generally always some kind of sulphide mineralisation associated with it. Large twinned crystals of arsenopyrite were very common, as were chalcopyrite and sphalerite crystals, but finding visible gold was always worthy of celebrations in the office.

All the core and RC logging was done on paper sheets and this was then hand drawn onto cross-sections on paper or plastic sheets. A draftsman was employed to do this although I would do the rough field copies as the drilling was being done. The draftsman did the final versions once all data had been collected for the drillholes (including assay results) and final collar locations were surveyed. Once computers became mainstream years later, all of this original drilling data was digitized into databases.

If I got a bit behind on the core logging I'd sometimes work on weekends to catch up. During the hot summer weather I took the opportunity to kill two birds with the one stone and got a bit of tanning done while working in the yard out the back of the exploration office. Thongs, sunglasses and a multi-purpose calico sample bag tied around my waist as an apron, was all the PPE (personal protective equipment) I needed, and required. PPE wasn't even a known acronym back then, let alone a mandatory requirement. In fact, the HR Manager and the Health and Safety Officer were all the one person – the "Secretary" – and there wasn't even one of these in the Exploration office in Bendigo.

The drill crews worked 12-hour days, 7 days a week but I only worked about 10 hours a day, Monday to Friday although weekend work was often necessary depending on the drilling operations. The drill crews stayed on the job for up to 12 weeks at a time, living out of a hotel in Eaglehawk.

On the weekends I'd quite often socialize with the drilling crews after they knocked off work for the day, joining them for beers and dinner at the hotel where they all stayed. All the drilling crews lived interstate in either Queensland or NSW and spent months away at a time from their home bases.

It wasn't long before I developed a special friendship with one of the drillers but our blossoming romance wasn't to last very long after he was told he was needed on a different project up in Queensland. After only a few months of getting to know each other he left town…and about a month later I packed up and joined him.

It was an agonizing decision to quit my job and I felt physically ill leading up to notifying my boss of my resignation. I loved the job but the love bug had bitten and it seemed it was time to follow my heart rather than my career for now.

Chapter 2

1984

LIVING IN DRILLING CAMPS

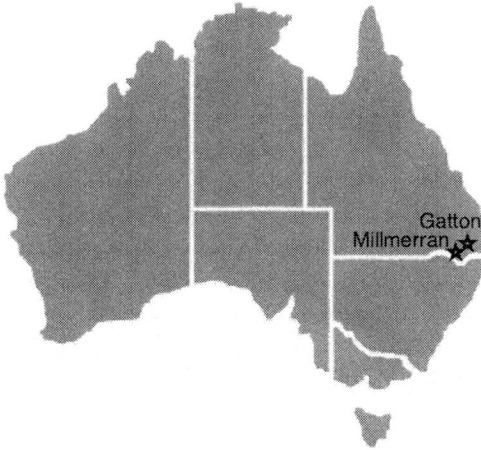

Gary was working for a drilling company called Rockdril Contractors and in the early eighties they started using mineral drilling rigs to drill slim-hole oil and gas wells. The initial rig used to pilot the system was Rockdril Rig #20 (Longyear 600) and Gary was chosen to be one of the drillers on this rig. The rig was elevated onto a sub-frame so a blowout preventer (BOP) could be installed in a cellar dug into the ground at the well location.

A conventional mineral drilling rig only has a crew of 2 or 3 workers (4 or 6 if there is to be night shift) but because of the 24-hour a day operations on an oil and gas rig, and the added manpower required in remote locations, this rig always travelled with a large transportable camp which would accommodate up to about 20 people. The camp was set up in close proximity to the rig and all people involved in the drilling program were based in the camp.

After finishing my job in Bendigo, I joined Gary in Queensland where Rig #20 was contracted to drill two wells in South East Queensland near Gatton and Millmerran. Gary had a caravan which we towed from his home base in Maryborough Qld, out to the drill site at Gatton, about 90 km (56 mi) west of Brisbane, and set up home next to the rig's transportable camp on the drill site lease. Two of the other drill crew members also had their girlfriends staying with them and we would all help do the cleaning and washing in the camp. The camp was fully self-sufficient, running off generators which provided power to run the camp and also the lights and workshop at the rig. The generators and the rig were powered with diesel, and water was pumped into a water truck and transported from a nearby dam.

In the 1980's there was no such thing as HR (Human Resources) or HS&E (Health Safety and Environment) departments. PPE (Personal Protective Equipment) was limited to steel capped work boots and hard hats although these weren't even strictly enforced. There were still plenty of small mineral rigs getting around with crews wearing baseball caps and thongs out on the rig.

With such long stints spent on the rig it was common to have girlfriends staying in the camps, so work became a way of life rather than just a job. Drinking beer and spirits after knocking off for the day was customary and this was quite often combined with the occasional bong around the campfire. There were definitely no alcohol or drug testing requirements back in those days. Considering I didn't drink spirits or do any sorts of drugs I still managed to fit in with the wayward group and hold my own in conversations with a common interest in drilling operations. Although I have to admit, I always had more in common with the men rather than the girlfriends, who generally had no interest in geology or drilling operations.

The well, Ropeley-1, was drilled for Queensland Petroleum Pty Ltd in the western margin of the Triassic Esk Trough and the overlying Jurassic Clarence-Moreton Basin. These two dominantly fluvial sedimentary basins lie within a Palaeozoic belt called the "Tasman Geosyncline". It was drilled to test a large surface mapped structure and to provide some reliable stratigraphic information. It was spudded on the 9th May 1984, rotary drilled to 220 m and then continuously diamond cored to a TD of 590 m. The core recovery was better than 99%.

A stratified and laminated sandstone interval from 459 to 520 m showed variable dull fluorescence with mostly poor streaming cut. The carbonaceous mudstone-shale potential source rocks had blotchy in situ orange fluorescence with a mostly good streaming cut. A siliceous sandstone unit from 463 to 468 m with moderate porosity and 36 md permeability was the most prospective reservoir unit encountered. The well was plugged and abandoned on the 27th May 1984.

Once that well was completed the entire camp was moved to the next location near Millmerran, about 120 km (75 mi) south west of Gatton, where the second well was then drilled.

Nangway-1 was spudded on the 30th May 1984 on the eastern margin of the Surat Basin, approximately 70 km (43 mi) east of the Moonie Oil Fields. The well was drilled to test a seismic defined Precipice Sandstone trap sealed by overlying Evergreen shales. It was rotary drilled to 252 m then continuously diamond cored to a total depth of 1075 m. The first 346 m of the well was drilled through the Jurassic Blythesdale Sandstone followed by the Walloon Coal measures down to 662 m. The Hutton Sandstone was drilled from 662 to 878 m with only minor methane gas encountered and this was followed by the Evergreen Shale and sandstone to 1050 m. The Precipice Sandstone was intersected from 1050 to 1068 m with only minor methane present, followed by the Triassic basement of talcose-altered volcanics and thin shales. Nangway-1 was plugged and abandoned on the 30th June 1984.

The rig and camp were then mobilized to the next location in the Northern Territory. Gary and I returned to Maryborough and dropped off the caravan and had a break for a week before driving up to meet the rig at the next wellsite on Bullo River Station in the far north western corner of the Northern Territory, a drive of over 3,600 km (2,237 mi).

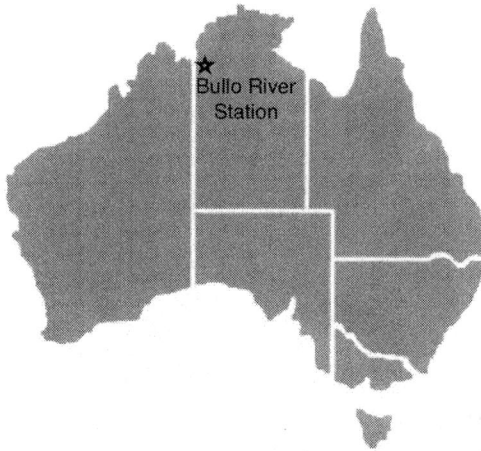

Bullo River
Station

We drove our own car up there while some of the drill crew drove up in the work Toyota's and trucks, and others flew up in a chartered plane that landed on the air strip at the Bullo River Station homestead, which was about 20 km (12 mi) from the drill site. Flying in and out of the station wasn't without its hazards, as some of the crew discovered when the light plane they were in struck a horse on the airstrip as they were taking off. One of the wings clipped the horse and the damage prevented the plane from being able to take off and it was left stranded on the property – along with the departing crew – until another plane could come in.

Bullo River Station is a cattle property (pastoral lease) spanning 1627 square kilometres (628 square miles) about 350 km (217 mi) south west of Darwin and 80 km (50 mi) north of Timber Creek. The Bullo River meanders for over 80 km through picturesque valley on the property, running from the freshwater Bullo Gorge to the saltwater tidal Victoria River, which also forms the eastern boundary of the property.

The station was then owned by American businessman and ex-serviceman Charles Henderson and his wife Sara. The couple had three teenage daughters who helped run the property and were schooled by School of the Air. Despite all three children of the couple being born and raised in Australia, they all spoke with American accents due to living in remote isolation with mainly their American father and Australian mother for social interaction. (*Side Note: Following Charles Henderson's death in 1986, and faced with significant debts, Sara and her daughters worked to turn the business around and to keep Bullo River Station. In 1990 Sara was named Australian Business Woman of the Year, which led to a publishing contract and a series of best-selling books which made Bullo River Station and the family's story famous across Australia and internationally*).

The drive to the drill site was on about 80 km (50 mi) of private property dirt road that left the Victoria Highway 30 km (19 mi) west of the small township of Timber Creek. This well had to be drilled in the "dry" season, between May and October, because in the wet season the roads are generally impassable.

We joined the rest of the crew at the site as the trucks were arriving with the rig and camp and it was all hands on deck to get everything set up. Everyone stayed on day shift while the camp was getting set up and worked until well after dark to get the transportable units and the rig offloaded from the trucks. The power wouldn't get hooked up to the dongas until the next day so everyone slept on mattresses out under the stars for the first night, as it was too hot in the dongas without the air conditioners operating. Dinner on the first night was a BBQ around a bonfire with everyone eating together for the only time until the campsite would be packed up again at the end of the drilling. The next night would see the crew split up into a day shift and night shift and 24-hour operations would begin.

The campsite was on the banks of a small tributary of the Bullo River and we were only metres away from the beautiful sandy banks and Pandanus palms that lined the clear water of the tropical tributary. If there was such a thing as an idyllic drill location – this was it.

Everyone worked 12-hour shifts every day for the duration of the well and would only get a break once the job was finished. There were a total of about 18 people in the camp, which included day shift and night shift cooks, drill crews, mud engineer, mudloggers and Geologist. Four of the crew members had their girlfriends in the camp and we helped with the cleaning and laundry.

Gary was working the midnight to midday shift and quite often we would take the small "tinny" that the station owners had lent us and row down the river through the magnificent Bullo Gorge for the afternoon. The weather was perfect every day – minimums of about 22°C and maximums of about 32°C (72 to 90°F) with clear blue skies.

We also had the odd visit from the Henderson girls and Bonny Henderson took some of us up in their light plane, performing aerobatic maneuvers over the remote landscape and low-level passes along the Bullo River. Bonnie would later go on to become a world champion in aerobatic flying and I certainly never underestimated her ability while I was flying upside down in the seat behind her – it was a highlight of our stay on their station.

Everyone slept in the transportable units ("dongas") and used the showers and toilets in an adjacent ablutions donga. There was also a recreation donga that had a TV for watching videos.

The day shift cook would do a fortnightly drive to the nearest town of Kununurra, about 300 km (186 mi) away, to replenish food and beer supplies and also get a load of videos. The food budget was pretty good so we never went without. This was our home for the next several weeks so everyone made the most of it. Our work and social lives were one and the same. Despite the drinking and smoking after shifts were finished for the day, there were never any problems with people not pulling their weight. Being a 24-hour operation meant that each shift couldn't knock off until their relief arrived so there was no way anyone could "sleep in" or "drop a shift".

The only method of communications with the office was by two-way radio. Satellite phones were still a few years off and there were no computers for data collection – all data was recorded by hand. Communications was by way of Codan two-way radios with "Scheds" to either the office in Brisbane or Alice Springs office at 0830 hrs and 1500 hrs each day. It quite often meant the supervisor had to drive to a place of higher ground where he could get the best radio reception.

Queensland Petroleum's Bullo River-1 well was drilled within the Proterozoic Victoria River Basin. It was spudded on the 15th July 1984 to test a large surface-mapped faulted structure. The hydrocarbon prospectivity of the area was relatively unknown but there were historical recordings of oil shows in the area and other Proterozoic rocks in the Northern Territory were showing signs of hydrocarbon presence.

A hole was rotary drilled to 250 m and then continuously cored to a TD of 970 m in the weakly altered graphic granite of the basement. There was no evidence of hydrocarbons while drilling and after drill stem tests and wireline logging were performed the well was plugged and abandoned on the 10th August 1984.

Once the drilling was completed everyone went onto day shift and we had an "end of well" BBQ down on the banks of the Bullo River, closer downstream to where it joins the Victoria River. The sandy banks were scarred with saltwater crocodile "slides" where the deadly reptiles had slid into the water. The cooks had even seen some in the area when they first arrived to start setting up for the BBQ.

With most people getting pretty drunk, it didn't take long before the first dare was called out for someone to swim across to the other side of the river. Being sober, I was mortified when someone took up the challenge and dived into the river and started thrashing their arms and legs around in an attempt to get to the other side. I practically held my breath as I watched dumbfounded as someone swam across the crocodile-infested river. I was fully expecting to see a big "salty" grab him and take him to the bottom of the river but fortunately he made it to the other side with no incident. Just as I started to breath again someone else jumped in and did the same. The fact that they both made it across and back without being taken by a croc was astounding and I was glad when they gave up on that game. The toolpusher, Col Olsen, was so scared that he was going to get thrown in that he disappeared and climbed up a tree and hid for a couple hours until it was time to go back to camp.

At the crack of dawn the next morning it was all hands on deck to start packing up the rig and load everything onto the waiting trucks. The camp got done the next day, which would then see everyone leaving, by either road or a light plane that was chartered to fly the remainder of the workers back to civilization. Gary and I started our long drive back to Maryborough where my home base was now at Gary's parents house – although we were only ever there for about one week every three months.

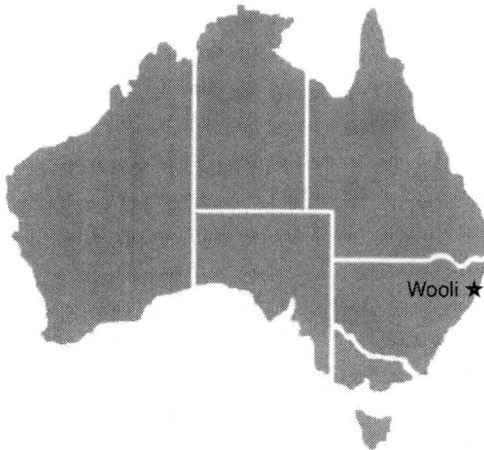

It only took eleven days from when they plugged and abandoned the well at Bullo River to when they spudded the next well, which was at Wooli, near the city of Grafton on the northern NSW coast. Gary and I had less than a week in Maryborough before hooking up the caravan again and driving down to Grafton to meet the trucks arriving with the rig and camp. It was pretty much the same crew that was on the last location so it was fun meeting up with everyone again and starting the process all over again. It was unusual to be drilling so close to a major city but we still lived in our donga camp, which was a short drive from the drill site.

This well, Pillar Valley-2, was being drilled for the Petroleum Section of the NSW Department of Mineral Resources as a fully cored stratigraphic hole in the southern Clarence-Moreton Basin. Drilling commenced on the 21st August 1984 and reached a total depth of 1,740 m

21

on the 13th October 1984. The well was spudded in possible Walloon Coal Measures, which continued for 121m then intersected 1,379 m of Bundamba Group before terminating in the Late Triassic Ipswich Coal Measures.

After seven weeks on this location the rig and camp were demobilized and we were excited to hear that the next drilling program for Rig #20 was to be in New Zealand and we eagerly awaited updates on who would be going over with the rig.

We were back in Maryborough on break when we finally got confirmation that Gary would be one of the drillers to go with the rig to NZ and I would be employed as a "campy" and would now get paid to do the cleaning and helping out with the kitchen duties – a job that was paid more generously than that of a graduate geologist. It would be a couple of months before we would be setting off though because of the delays in getting the rig prepared for the strict customs requirements for the boat trip over the Tasman Sea. Gary and I would eventually witness the loading of the rig at the wharf in Brisbane and soon after we flew to New Zealand, on the west coast of the South Island, which would be our home on-and-off for the next 20 months.

Chapter 3

1985-1986

DRILLING IN NEW ZEALAND

★ Moana

Once all the crew arrived in Greymouth we picked up the hired vehicles and drove out to where our base would be in Moana, on the shores of Lake Brunner. We arrived on New Year's Eve in 1984-1985 and with the rig still not arrived we had time to relax and enjoy the amazing scenery at our new home. After a night of seeing the New Year in (like only a drill crew with no work to do the next day can do!) a swim in the near freezing Lake Brunner on New Year's morning bought some sobriety back into the crews. With the dust settled on the previous nights festivities the story of the day was how one of the roustabouts, Clarky, thought he was onto a good thing at the bar of the local pub when he managed to get a kiss out of an attractive lady who was showing him some attention. After talking to some of the locals it was discovered the "she" was actually a "he" and Clarky had kissed a boy! It turns out there was an unproportunately high number of transsexuals in the Moana area and one of them just happened to be this attractive lady, Donna. And then there was also the local pig farmer who was built like an All Blacks halfback, had hands the size of baseball mitts and a voice deeper than Gary's. We were never sure if she'd actually had the "cut and tuck" done but she went by the name of "Jacqui" (or was it Jackie?) and obviously wanted to be a woman, so Jacqui she was.

We set up camp in a local hostel-style accommodation perched up on the side of a hill overlooking Moana and the picturesque lake Brunner and Southern Alps. The budget accommodation house had several rooms that slept eight people in bunk beds. They were very basic rooms with bare concrete floors (which fortunately had heating within the slab) and pine framework bunks lining each side of the room. Gary and I had a room to ourselves and other workers shared rooms with 4 men in each room. I was the only female to travel from Australia as all the other men who had their girlfriends on the rig in Australia were sent to work on other rigs in Australia. Only a few of the original Rig #20 crew were to make the trip so we were pretty excited about making the cut.

The kitchen was equally as sparse as the bedrooms and was a huge room also with bare concrete floors and crudely constructed pine tables and benches. Despite the bare-bones lodgings there was an upside – the views over the lake and beyond to the Southern Alps was breathtaking.

The first well drilled in New Zealand was close to Lake Brunner, which is why we stayed in Moana first up. We were drilling for New Zealand Oil and Gas (NZOG) and the first well, Arnold River-1, which was spudded on the 6th January 1985, was drilled to investigate the interpretation of existing seismic and well data indicating the presence of a Late Eocene sandstone with good reservoir potential. The well location was 3 km southwest of the Kotuku oil seep, which is the largest known natural occurrence of petroleum in New Zealand which rises to the surface and pools on the ground.

The Arnold River play was interpreted to be primarily dependent on fault sealing against the upthrown Kotuku block but this well was unsuccessful in finding any notable hydrocarbons and was plugged and abandoned as a dry well on the 18th January 1985.

Another two wells were drilled in the same area. Taipo Creek-1 was spudded on the 22nd January 1985 roughly 2.5 km south of the Kotuku oil seep. This well was plugged and abandoned as a dry well on the 31st January 1985. The third well was Mawhera-1, which was spudded on the 4th February 1985 at a distance of about 3.5 km from the Kotuku oil seep. It was also plugged and abandoned as a dry well on the 18th February 1985.

After a six-week hitch in New Zealand, Gary and I took a two-week break and flew back to Maryborough and got married. After a week-long honeymoon on Hayman Island we headed back to New Zealand and settled into a three month hitch that would see us starting at a new location in the small town of Ohai, in the Southland region of the South Island, 65km (40 miles) northwest of Invercargill, the most southerly city in New Zealand.

✩ Ohai

We set up camp in two old rented houses that had the bare minimum comforts, as usual. Fortunately it wasn't quite winter yet so the weather wasn't as cold as it could have been, but it was still a lot colder than what we were used to back home. The lush green pastoral fields were testament to high annual rainfall and cold conditions. Ohai not only had the greenest grass but also the whitest sheep I had ever seen – again a sure sign this place never saw any dust and heat.

The houses we were renting had ancient electrical wiring and every time someone used the toaster in the kitchen it would trip all the power in the house. The small electrical fan heaters that everyone had in their rooms wouldn't have helped with the power problems either.

The only form of entertainment was again VHS videos, which were watched on a TV in the lounge room of the main house. There was usually an even mix of general viewing movies and porn movies, all of which I would have to source from a video shop in Invercargill. At the time it was common for most video shops to have porn movies hidden out the back of the shop and you just had to ask discreetly if you could select from their "private collection" out the back. No drilling camp was complete in the 80's without posters of nude women plastered all over the walls, porn movies showing on the TV, alcohol consumption from dinner to bedtime and the occasional bong thrown in. It was definitely a male domain and the comraderie amongst the crews would quite often cement life-long friendships and form the basis of a lifestyle that, for many, was difficult to give up.

There was generally at least one strong personality amongst the crew that created the morale for the entire camp. Eno, the camp cook, was that person. He'd been on Rig #20 since I had joined the crew with Gary and his fun personality rubbed off onto everyone – it was hard to be angry when Eno was on the job. Thirty years later we are still mates and stay in touch and reminisce about the old times on Rig #20.

Like Greymouth, Ohai was a coal mining town. This program was a five well Coal Bed Methane (CBM) program for the company "South Gas". Two wells were drilled directly into the coal seams whilst two were planned to intersect old underground mine drives. Several wells had excellent gas flows and it was deemed a very successful campaign. The whole town turned up for the initial flare lighting ceremony, which ended in an all night party.

Once the wells in Ohai were completed, the rig was

packed up and transported to Patea, on the North Island, in the oil-rich region of Taranaki. We drove up in the hired minibus and work Toyotas, driving through the most amazing scenery up the entire length of the South Island.

It was coming into winter now so the Southern Alps (which ran for much of the length of the South Island) were snow-capped and a majestic sight during our drive up north. The road trips were always a lot of fun and gave everyone a break from the hard 12-hour shifts during drilling operations.

We again set up our base from two rented houses in Patea and the crew drove the 10 km to the rig which was drilling on a lease near Hawera, which was half way to New Plymouth.

The well was drilled to test an anticlinal drape structure expressed in Pliocene sediments overlying the Patea

Basement High. The well was spudded on the 15th April 1985 with the top of the prospective Matemateaonga Formation encountered at 338.5 m. Sandstones with good reservoir properties were present but were entirely fresh water bearing. There were no significant gas peaks or hydrocarbon shows. On the 19th May 1985 the well was plugged and abandoned as a dry well.

As a bonus to the local community, no top plug was placed so the Taranaki Catchment Commission could complete the bore as a water well.

Once the well near Patea was finished we flew back home to Maryborough for a two-week break. By the time we returned to New Zealand the rig was drilling back near Greymouth and we returned to find the camp now based out of a holiday (caravan) park along the beach near Greymouth. We rented rooms and also a cabin that had a kitchen, which we used as the hub for our camp. The small kitchen was less than ideal after having a commercial-style kitchen in the normal drilling camps but we had to make do with what we had at our disposal.

The holiday park was 5 km (3 miles) south of Greymouth city at South Beach, and was along the foreshore of the Tasman Sea coastline. Compared to Australian beaches this beach was very ordinary with poorly sorted greyish sand, and combined with the unfavourable weather, it was anything but inviting. But, like in Moana, the consolation prize was that we looked south down along the length of the magnificent Southern Alps. It was still summer time so the weather wasn't too cold and the Southern Alps only had minor snow-capped peaks showing.

There was also the incredible "Greymouth Barber" which is a notorious, chilly wind that streams down the Grey Valley in the morning, funneled through the Grey River gap, and marked by a trail of white mist. It is locally known as 'the barber', reputedly because it cuts you to the bone. The sight of this low-level cloud mass streaming down along the river and pouring out into the sea was captivating.

With winter fast approaching, the colder weather meant the Greymouth Barber was a common occurrence and from the beach foreshore of our accommodation we had a fantastic view of the mist spilling out of the Grey River mouth into the Tasman Sea.

The daytime temperatures sometimes barely reached above freezing point quite often and puddles of water on the drill site were frozen to ice and never melted for days. With the crews working "midnight to midday" or "midday to midnight" it meant that everyone had at least 8 hours of working in the dark and freezing overnight temperatures. The daylight hours were short and with most of the drilling being done in the shadow of the Southern Alps it meant there was only a few hours of sunlight each day. But of course, this is the "Land of the Long White Cloud" which meant that clear blue skies were a rarity anyway.

While we were drilling these wells Gary developed glandular fever and his throat became so swollen he was admitted to hospital where he was put under general anesthetic to lance his severely swollen tonsils. He spent another week recuperating in the camp but soon returned back to his 12-hour shifts standing in the freezing cold conditions at the rig site in the foothills of the Southern Alps.

The Greymouth region had a strong history of coal mining since the mid-1800's. Unfortunately though, it also had a bad record of coal mining fatalities, which was attributed to the complex structural geology that destabilized the coal seams once they were intersected during underground mining.

The first of the wells to be drilled back down on the west coast of the South Island was Kumara-2 for the Petroleum Corporation of NZ (PetroCorp), which was spudded on the 25th May 1985.

Kumara-2 was drilled as an exploration well to evaluate the Kumara Structure that had been intersected in the previously drilled Kumara-1 well. Cores from the Brunner and Paparoa coal measures had poor oil shows within the sandstones and core analysis indicated poor reservoir properties. At 1,756 m the drill string became stuck and Kumara-2A was kicked-off at 1523 m and re-drilled the section to a total depth of 1,771 m. Following testing the well was plugged and abandoned on the 3rd September 1985.

On another 2-week break back to Australia, we planned to start with a visit to my family in Melbourne and then head up to Maryborough for the remainder of the break. While departing Christchurch airport in a Boeing 747 our plane struck a flock of birds on take off which resulted in two of the four engines being inoperable. An emergency landing had to be made but not before we circled over the ocean off the coast of Christchurch while the pilots released the bulk of the fuel in the wing tanks as the plane is too heavy to pull up on the runway if it has full fuel tanks which add a considerable weight, and therefore momentum, to the plane.

As if in a scene out of a movie, I watched out the window as we came down to land and saw fire engines lining the runway and spectators cars lining the perimeter of the airport waiting to see the emergency landing, that was obviously broadcast over the news in the city as the drama was unfolding up in the air.

We managed to pull up safely but took the whole length of the runway to stop because they were unable to use the flaps to slow down after touching down because of the two engines that weren't operating. Uneven braking power from either side of the plane would have resulted in us spinning out of control on the runway so the pilot had to basically rely solely on the brakes.

We were towed from the end of the runway to the terminal building where we had to remain seated on the plane for a couple of hours while the airport authority decided what to do with us. They had to figure out if they could get a replacement plane to take us that night or if we would have to stay in Christchurch overnight and leave the next day. At any rate, the departure lounge was already full of people from another flight so we had to wait until that was cleared before they would let us off the plane. We eventually got to leave later that night and safely made it to Melbourne.

After a 2-week break back in Australia we returned to New Zealand and met up with the rig, which was now back drilling near Greymouth again. Our return trip was not without plane incidents as well. We flew back to Wellington on the North Island and it took three attempts in a charter plane before we finally successfully took off and headed for Greymouth. The planes instruments weren't showing what they were meant to so each time we started taxiing to take off, we'd have to return to the hanger and get things sorted out before we could try again.

Our camp was set up back in the cabins at Moana in order to be closer to the sites of the next wells, which would be drilled for New Zealand Oil and Gas. It was now September but the weather was still freezing and the site of the Southern Alps covered in snow for as far as the eye could see down south was amazing.

The first well back at this location was Glenn Creek-1, which was spudded on the 14th September 1985 and cored to obtain stratigraphic data. It was plugged and abandoned on the 27th September 1985.

Following the three well program we had done for NZOG earlier in the year near the Kotuku oil seep, a seismic program was conducted over the area southwest of the Kotuku Dome. Evaluation of this, along with the previous drilling results, suggested possible thrust fault-controlled flexure in the Paleogene and Cretaceous sediments. The next well we drilled, Niagara-1, would help consolidate the stratigraphic information and test for these structures. Evaluation of the zones of interest indicated some moveable oil in thick turbidite sandstones. After conducting two drill stem tests with encouraging results the well was suspended on the 30th October pending further testing.

It was time for another break and instead of flying back to Australia for our 2-week break we decided to rent a car and drive around the North Island of New Zealand. As a driller, Gary was entitled to get his airfares paid to return to his home base of Maryborough after every 3-month hitch so we organized for Rockdril to pay for our rental car hire for two weeks in lieu of his airfare home and we spent our break sightseeing in New Zealand.

At the end of our break we met back up with the rig, which by now was starting a new well near Murchison on the northern end of the South Island.

☆ Murchison

We set up camp in the Riverside Holiday Park on the banks of the beautiful Buller River where we lived in small cabins and used the large communal kitchen for meal times. We spent Christmas and New Year at this site and enjoyed the amazing seasonal fruit of New Zealand's premier fruit growing area in Nelson. There was lots to see and do in the area and despite working 12-hour days we still managed to spend some time sightseeing and of particular interest was the site of the 1929 Murchison earthquake. It occurred on the White Creek Fault, located in the Buller Gorge, resulting in a large surface fault rupture visible in the Buller River, indicating about 4.5 m of vertical movement and 2.5 m of lateral movement. The area is also renowned for white-water rafting and we enjoyed a visit to nearby thermal pools nestled in a deep valley of lush rainforest.

The Matiri-1 well was drilled for PetroCorp to test the

sandstone stringers of the Brunner Coal Measures on the Matiri Anticline. The Te Wiriki Anticline is a sub-thrust closure comprising of a series of small fault independent closures with larger fault dependent potential. Tight gas had been identified in reservoirs that comprise the Brunner Coal Measures and Nuggety Sandstone, the Matiri Formation and the Tutaki graded sandstones of the lower Mangles Formation.

This well was outside the Murchison permit but was significant as a result of the detailed documentation and full stratigraphic record the well presented. Gas shows occurred within the Brunner and overlying Kaiata Mudstone. Several intervals on the well were tested. A moderate flow in one test and poor tests on several other zones resulted in only minor gas flows. The coals and mudstones were generally considered too tight to produce.

After completing the well in Murchison we had a period of downtime while we were waiting on confirmation of where the rig would be going next. We had our camp based out of Moana again and a skeleton crew of Gary and myself and the rig mechanics were kept on to caretake and do any maintenance on the rig.

It was during this time that I developed bad abdominal pains and after a couple of days of it not getting any better I started to suspect I may have had appendicitis so I went to a doctor in Greymouth to get it checked out. To my surprise the doctor diagnosed that I was most likely suffering from an ectopic pregnancy and she organized for me to have an ultrasound at the Greymouth hospital, which confirmed her diagnosis. I was immediately scheduled for surgery and was operated on later that day to have the offending fallopian tube removed.

Gary and I had been planning to start a family so it was a disappointment that our first attempt was a failure. After a couple of nights spent in the Greymouth Hospital I returned to the camp in Moana. Fortunately we were still just in caretaking mode so I didn't need to cook and clean after the full rig crew.

We eventually secured another contract to drill one final well for NZOG. Hohunu-1 was located 28 km southeast of Greymouth and 500 m west of Lake Brunner. After the discovery of producible oil in the Mid Miocene turbidite sandstones in Niagara-1, further seismic was acquired to detail the Niagara Structure and the Hohonu Lead. Hohonu-1 was drilled to test these structures but the well proved unsuccessful because of the lack of reservoir development in the main objective of the Niagara Sandstone Member.

Soon after this the rig was demobilized and in August 1986 it was left in storage at Tom Crofts Transport yard in Stillwater, about half way between Moana and Greymouth. After stacking the rig we flew back to Australia.

After returning to Australia, Gary had a couple of weeks off at home before heading back to work on other rigs in remote locations but I chose to stay at home. By this stage we had bought our own home and it wasn't long before I discovered I was pregnant again and this time it was a keeper!

Chapter 4

1987

FAMILY LIFE IN A DESERT CAMP

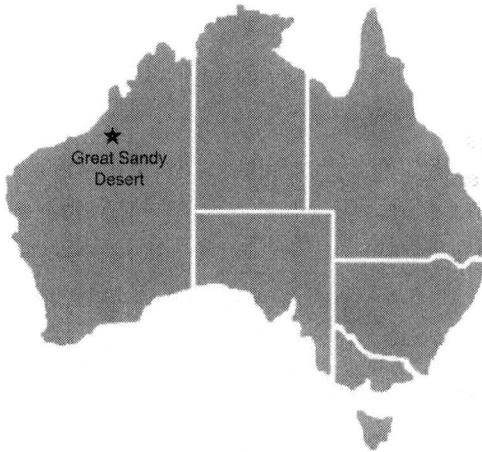

Most of my pregnancy was spent at home although I spent a few weeks out on location with Gary on mineral drilling jobs where he was staying in any towns that had decent accommodation. He was now back to working roughly 12-week hitches with 2-week breaks, flying or driving from the rig sites in the Northern Territory, Western Australia and northern Queensland back to our home base in Maryborough, Queensland.

Our first baby was due in early July of 1987 and for the last few months of the pregnancy I was carrying the baby in a breach position so I was scheduled for a cesarean section delivery, which made it a bit easier for Gary to time his break and be home for it. I attended the antenatal classes on my own but made some close friends with ladies who would be having their babies around the same time as me. I have to admit though; I felt more like a bored unemployed geologist than a clucky mother-to-be. In fact, I think right up until I had my first baby I had never even held a baby before! Other peoples new born babies looked pretty damn ugly to me to tell you the truth. Despite this, I was looking forward to having my own baby and knew I would feel maternal towards my own flesh and blood once the time arrived.

Despite not being involved in any gym training I still remained active throughout my pregnancy. I didn't suffer from any morning sickness and felt great all the way through the pregnancy.

Gary arrived home two days before my scheduled delivery date and the cesarean section went according to plan. I delivered a healthy 5lb 11oz baby boy who we named Christopher.

After his usual 2-week break, Gary went back to work for another 12-week hitch, leaving Christopher and me at home. I think I probably found it easier just having a baby to look after instead of a baby and an adult, and I managed to cope with the sleepless nights OK, despite there being no 24-hour TV, or even radio, back in those days so the night feeds were pretty quiet and boring.

Gary's first break home since the birth was when Christopher was 3 months old. He would be going back to work on Rockdril Rig #20 in a camp in the Great Sandy Desert in northern Western Australia, about 290km south east of Broome, and we decided that all three of us would drive over in our own car and stay in the camp for his next

3-month hitch. We had traded in Gary's V-8 panel van for a more family-friendly station wagon and packed what little gear we would need for the 5-day, nearly 5,000km (3,100 miles) drive to the rig site.

It was early October when we left and it was already getting very hot in the outback the further north we travelled. We soon realized the air conditioner in the car was not able to keep up with the extreme temperatures during the middle of the day so we had to revert to winding the windows down and putting up with the wind and heat. Christopher was still 100% breast fed at this stage so travelling with a 3-month-old baby was very easy, all we needed to carry for him were disposable nappies and "00"-sized singlets, no other clothes would be needed where we were going.

On the afternoon of the 5th day of travel and 185 km south of Broome, we finally turned inland off the Great Northern Highway, and headed along a sand track for the 90km drive to the rig site on Nita Downs station. As we needed to travel with the windows down due to the ineffective air-conditioner in the car, by the time we arrived at the camp Christopher was covered in a fine layer of red dust. Being the happy traveller he was, he didn't seem to mind and slept for most of the journey.

The CRA-supplied camp was already set up with several demountable units (dongas) which housed the kitchen and eating mess, recreation room, showers, toilets, laundry and bedrooms. Each room had a noisy box air-conditioner mounted in a hole in the wall and two spring-based single beds with thin foam mattresses. There was about 1 metre of space between the two beds with a table positioned under the window and a tall narrow clothes cabinet at the end of each bed just inside the door. Being a 24-hour operation the rooms usually had a day-shift person and their night-shift relief housed in the same room so there was usually only one person sleeping in the room at any one time. The windows were always covered with aluminium foil to prevent light from entering for the night shift workers who had to sleep during the day.

A dam was built by digging a huge hole in the ground about 100 metres from the accommodation and lined with plastic. Groundwater was pumped from a bore and stored in the dam and this was then pumped to the camp and used for both showers and the kitchen. There was no bottled water back then so bore water was our only option for potable drinking water – or beer, spirits and soft drink! Fortunately the bore water was very fresh and beautiful drinking water.

Gary was now a supervisor on the rig (tool pusher) and we had a room to ourselves with a single bed on one side of the room and a mattress on the floor on the other side of the room for Christopher. Our room was in-between two other rooms which only had thin plywood walls - which meant I had to make sure Christopher *never* cried while he was in the room. The last thing shift workers who had worked a 12-hour shift in 40+ degree heat in the middle of the Great Sandy Desert wanted was to have their sleep disturbed by a crying baby.

The one new feature at this campsite was the addition of a "hi-tech" Telstra satellite phone – well, it was hi-tech for its day! You may not have been able to carry it around in your hip pocket but at least we felt more connected to the rest of the world now. It goes without saying that the calls were extremely expensive and kept to a minimum – mostly for daily reports to town with updates on the progress of the drilling. The phone was mounted on the trailer itself so you had to stand next to the satellite dish to make a phone call – there was nothing mobile about this phone. We also had a fax machine hooked up to it so all the drilling reports could now be faxed to town on a daily basis.

Despite our nomadic-style camp, we were just like thousands of other families who lived in the Australian "outback" – only these people had to deal with the social isolation all their lives. It was a humbling experience to get out of the city for a few months and survive without the conveniences of life that everyone takes for granted. The people who live on the vast stations in Northern Australia had only 2-way radios for communications, education and medical needs. The children were educated via radio through the "School of the Air" and any medical emergencies were taken care of by the "Royal Flying Doctor Service". While our drilling camp was a "mere" 290 km from the nearest town of Broome, some of Australia's families live several hundreds of kilometres from a supermarket and these property owners generally own their own light aircraft and have a dirt landing strip on their property so they can fly to the nearest town to stock up on supplies. We considered ourselves lucky to be only a 7-hour round trip drive away from a supermarket!

****

Rig #20 had arrived back to Brisbane from New Zealand in April 1987 and soon after was mobilised to Sandy Camp.

The drilling program consisted of four vertical diamond drillholes, DD87SS04, DD87SS05, DD87SS06 and DD87SS07 for CRA Exploration. Mud rotary pre-collars were used to drill the cover sequence and manage zones of artesian water and gas kicks. The drillholes were further investigating the resource potential of the Admiral Bay Project, which was discovered in 1981 by Meridian Oil NL during petroleum exploration, and was subsequently acquired by CRA Exploration (the exploration arm of CRA Limited, now Rio Tinto Ltd).

The Admiral Bay Project is located in the central Canning Basin, on the southern edge of the Kimberley region some 140 km south of Broome, Western Australia. Admiral Bay lies within the Admiral Bay Fault Zone, which separates the Broome Platform and Willara Sub basin of the Canning Basin. Within the project area, the surface geology is dominated by Quaternary Aeolian sand. Sand sheets in the northwest grade into 2–10m high dunes towards the southeast. *(The Admiral Bay deposit undertook substantial exploration from 1986 to 1992. Kagara Ltd acquired the deposit from CRA Exploration in 2004 and completed an exploration program that lead to an initial Inferred Resource, as well as a prefeasibility study to test the viability of the project. Kagara Ltd entered into Administration in 2012 and subsequently Liquidation in 2013.)*

Diamond core drilling over several drilling campaigns undertaken by CRA Exploration Pty Ltd and by Kagara Ltd. have since identified the following geological information:

· Admiral Bay is carbonate-hosted zinc-lead-silver-barium deposit, with mineralisation hosted mainly in the Nita Formation and, to a lesser degree, in the Carribuddy and Goldwyer Formations, over a mineralised strike extent of at least 18km; nominally the deposit is classified as a Mississippi Valley Type deposit (MVT).

· The stratigraphy is comprised of a thick sequence of Cretaceous-Jurassic-Permian sandstones/siltstones (up to 1,200m thick), which overlies a variably dolomitised siltstone/shale/limestone – the Nita Formation – which is host to an upper zinc-rich zone and a lower lead-rich zone of mineralization.

· Sulphides infill dissolution, breccia and fracture porosity and overprint stylolites.

· Previous drilling indicates that the upper high-grade Zn-rich zone is up to 20m thick, whilst the lower highgrade Pb zone is up to 15m thick. The high-grade zones described above are hosted within a broad, moderately Zn-Pb mineralised, zone up to 110-120m thick.

· In general, base metal mineralisation occurs in the lower parts of the Siluro-Devonian Caribuddy Formation and the Ordovician-age Nita and Goldwyer Formations over depths of around 1,250m to 1,700m. Mineralisation is most typically associated with calcareous rocks, commonly with appreciable barite. The mineralised zones at Admiral Bay are approximately tabular and flat lying to shallowly dipping, at a nominal depth of 1,350m below the surface.

· Mineralisation is generally intersected with near true width down hole lengths. Five individual mineralised zones were interpreted. The zones are currently interpreted to be coincident with an antiformal structure associated with the Admiral Bay Fault Zone.

****

We lived in this camp for 3 months, until the 1987 drilling campaign was completed. Everyone worked 12 hours a day for the entire 12 weeks, in temperatures that ranged from 40 to 50 degrees Celsius (104-122°F) every day. I used the white foam boxes that the vegetables came in as a bathtub for Christopher and also as a swimming pool for cooling off in during the middle of the day. Every couple of weeks when the cook went to town to get another load of food and supplies I would put an order in for disposable nappies. By the time we left the camp Christopher was also eating small amounts of solid food but mostly still just breastfed. To make sure he never cried in our room I had to lay down with him until he fell asleep and then keep checking on him regularly to make sure he hadn't woken up.

The wellsite was about 300m from the campsite and the crew would have their lunch taken up to them and it was eaten on the run, as the rig was never shut down. With black, greasy hands the crew would eat their sandwiches in one hand while still working on the job - the full twelve-hour shift was spent working.

The crew worked from midday to midnight or midnight to midday and the supervisors and geologist worked from 6am to 6pm. The people knocking off at 6pm usually had trouble having a shower after work as the water stored in the tanks at the bathroom would have heated up so much during the day that it would be scorching coming out of the taps. There was a shower set up next to the dam which had water pumped directly from the dam which had slightly cooler water because of the large volume it contained.

While we were on location Gary managed to take our car to Broome and get a larger air-conditioner fitted to it so we could use it on the drive home as it was going to be much hotter than the drive over three months earlier.

Once the drilling of the wells was completed, a convoy of trucks arrived to start the de-mobilisation of the rig and camp back to the Rockdril base in Alice Springs. The last day on site is always a very long one and by the end of it there's no power or water as the generators get packed up and loaded onto the trucks with all the other gear.

Although we were driving home in our own car, Gary had to remain close to the convoy of trucks and crew who were driving the Rockdril vehicles so he could supervise the demobilization. It was now December and the temperatures were around 50°C every day while driving over to the Northern Territory. We were very grateful to have a cool car to drive in and I felt sorry for all the crew who were driving work vehicles with no working air conditioners and had to keep the windows partly wound up because the blast of hot air coming in while they were driving on the highway was too hot to tolerate. After two days on the road escorting the convoy of Rockdril vehicles and trucks we finally went our own way at the "Threeways", where the trucks continued heading south to Alice Springs, which was 520km away, and we headed east on the Barkly Highway towards Queensland. We still had another two days of driving to go before we would finally get back home to Maryborough.

Chapter 5

1988

TODDLER IN THE CAMP

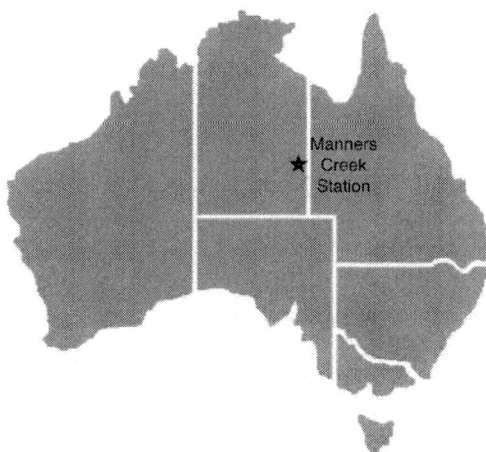

Gary returned to work after a few weeks off over the Christmas-New Year period and I stayed at home in Maryborough with Christopher, who was now six months old. After two more 12-week hitches away Gary was home for Christopher's first birthday on the 1st July. By this stage Rig #20 was drilling on a cattle station near the border of the Northern Territory and Queensland and we decided on all going out there when Gary returned.

The nearest "town" to where the rig campsite was set up was Urandangi, which was about an hour's drive along a dirt road across the border into Queensland. Urandangi is located on the banks of the Georgina River and is 187 km (116 miles) south west of the regional centre of Mount Isa and 2,000 km (1247 miles) north west of the Queensland capital city of Brisbane. The township was founded in 1885 as a centre for travellers and drovers where a stock route crossed the Georgina River. By 1920 Urandangi had a pub, two stores, post office, police station and a dance hall but now its only major facility is the Urandangi Hotel, or the "Dangi Pub", and a small state school that services the surrounding indigenous community.

We decided against driving this time and Rockdril paid for all of us to fly from Maryborough to Alice Springs, via Brisbane and Sydney, and then we had a small chartered Cessna that took us out to the remote camp location.

This would be Christopher's first FIFO trip to a rig and it should have come as no surprise to us that 17 years later he would be working FIFO to drilling camps himself.

We landed on the airstrip at Manners Creek cattle station, a pastoral lease of just under 8,090 square kilometres (3,124 square miles) on the Northern Territory side of the state border. A Rockdril vehicle met us when we landed and drove us back to the Rig #20 camp.

Gary had a caravan which doubled as his office and it also meant we had a much more comfortable place to stay as a family compared to the small single bed we had in the little donga during our last visit to the rig.

Christopher was now a toddler and a very happy-go-lucky kid who loved the attention he got from all the drill crew. He always had a smile on his face and he was proof that kids don't need expensive toys to keep them occupied.

Being the middle of winter, the daytime temperatures were usually around a pleasant 30°C (86°F) and a coolish 10°C (50°F) at night. Despite the mild temperature, flies were in plague proportions and were extremely annoying when you were outside.

In addition to the flies we also had to contend with very poor quality bore water that tasted dreadful. It was always a huge treat when the cook came back from his shopping trip to Mount Isa with containers of fresh town water. Most people chose to drink soft drinks or beer, which were both in plentiful supply.

The Iterra satellite phone was now a permanent feature of the rig camp, which made us look very hi-tech out in the middle of nowhere.

Although Manners Creek station was in the Northern Territory, the wellsite was located 10 km east of the Northern territory-Queensland border and 65 km SSW of Urandangi.

The well, Bradley-1, was the second of three stratigraphic wells drilled by Pacific Oil and Gas Pty Ltd (POG) during the company's 1988 Georgina Basin drilling program. The well was designed to assess the eastern portion of the Palaeozoic Georgina Basin for its potential for commercial quantities of hydrocarbons by determining the distribution, thickness and quality of source and reservoir rock facies and to provide good lithologic and geophysical control in an area where little stratigraphic or other data was available.

The well was spudded on the 6th July 1988 and rotary drilled to a depth of 504 m then continuously diamond cored from 504 m to a total depth of 904.4 m after intersecting Pre-Cambrian granite at a depth of 886 m. Drilling was stopped almost 400 m short of its anticipated depth as Cambrian sediments had thinned significantly from what they were expecting from a previously drilled offset well 84 km south of Bradley-1 location. All the formations penetrated were high to prognosis and thinner than predicted with the expected Thorntonia Limestone and Late Proterozoic sediments were completely absent due to onlap over the basement high present at this location.

Several traces of oil shows were encountered throughout the prospective zones however they were usually confined to very thin laminations, individual vugs or thin sub-vertical fractures and were generally discontinuous and less than a few centimetres in thickness.

The well was plugged and abandoned on the 11th August 1988.

The camp was then moved to Tarlton Downs station, a 3,034 square kilometre (1,171 square miles) cattle station in the far eastern Northern Territory. Despite the harshness of the environment and the long days spent on the rig, the crew still maintained high spirits and indulged in the customary "throwing the Wellsite Geologist in the sump" (and anyone else who they cared to throw in at the time).

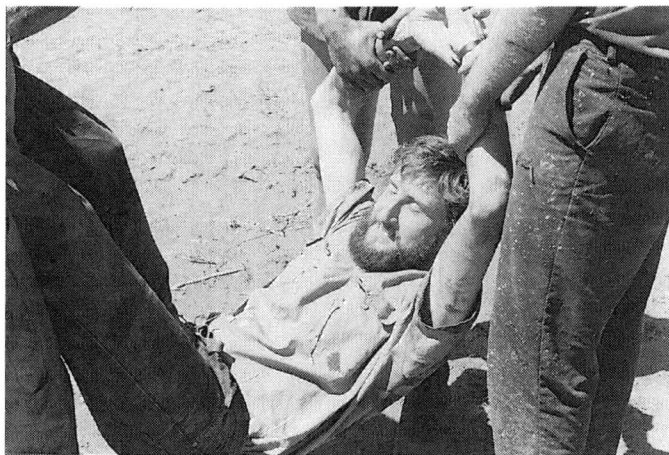

Hacking-1 was spudded on the 11th August 1988 close to the southern margin of the Georgina Basin. The top section of the well was rotary drilled to 251 m and then continuously diamond cored to a total depth of 1234 m after intersecting granite basement at 1222 m, which was 434 m higher than prognosed. Although minor scattered gas shows and hydrocarbon odour was encountered, drill stem tests and wireline logging confirmed it to be a dry well and it was plugged and abandoned on the 18th September 1988.

With the well completed it was time to begin the demobilization and travel to the next well site, which would be about 1,300 km (808 miles) away at the northern end of the Northern Territory. While the rig was in the final stages of getting loaded onto the trucks, Christopher and I left the camp with one of the cooks who was a girlfriend of one of the drillers. We started out in their Landcruiser along the sandy dirt access road, heading for the Plenty Highway. Unfortunately we got a flat tyre along the way so Vicki and I had to change it before continuing.

The Plenty Highway is a 498 km (310 miles) mostly unsealed road in the Northern Territory that begins at a turnoff from the Stuart Highway 68 km north of Alice Springs and finishes at Tobermorey Homestead on the

Northern Territory/Queensland border. The first 100 km from the Stuart Highway is sealed while the remainder of it is red dirt.

It took us two days to travel the distance, staying overnight in a roadhouse hotel along the way, and travelling north along the Stuart Highway up the centre of the Northern Territory to Daly Waters where we then left the highway and headed east along a dirt road for the remainder of the trip to the campsite on Nutwood Downs station.

We were on another hot and dusty lease in the middle of nowhere although we felt a bit more tethered to civilization than we were on the last location – we at least had a roadhouse and a pub within 30 km of our campsite and the nearest town of Katherine was only about 300 km (186 miles) "up the road."

The convoy of trucks followed us into the area that had been pre-cleared for our set-up of the rig and camp and it was all hands on deck to help offload all the gear. Generally the camp gear got offloaded first and everyone helped get it set up so there was somewhere to sleep at the end of the day. With the donga's lifted into place, the plumbing and electrical equipment was installed in preparation for getting the power and water up and running. The next step was to start up the generator but unfortunately there was a problem with it and the mechanic was unable to get it started. All trouble-shooting efforts to get it started failed which resulted in us having no power for the next 24 hours until it could be fixed.

With no power, we also had no water because it had to be pumped from the water tank to the ablution block. And of course we had no refrigeration, no air conditioners, no kettle, and once nighttime arrived – no lights! The only way to have a wash was under the water trucks outlet pipe at the back of the truck but that just had to do for today.

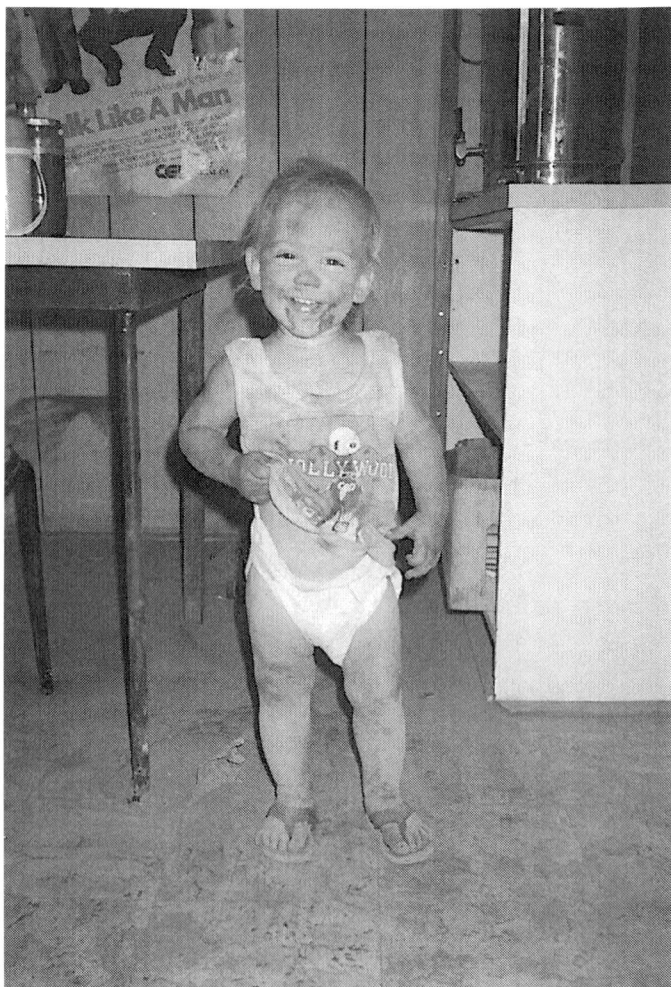

Christopher had a ball playing in the dirt while I was helping set the kitchen and camp up with the crew and wasn't at all concerned about the lack of modern day comforts that even a remote drilling camp would usually have.

Within 48 hours we got the generator problems sorted, the camp and rig sites set up and commenced drilling the well. Everyone settled into their 12-hour shifts and the routine started all over again.

On one of the cook's trips to Katherine to get supplies he came across a truck that had overturned on the highway and all the contents of the container he was carrying were spilled out across the highway. The goods were heading to a Kmart store and because they were now damaged they were going to be written off in an insurance claim so the cook and his offsider filled up what space was remaining in the Landcruiser with the discarded goods. To everyone's amusement he came back to camp with boxes of thongs (Jandals), summer pyjamas, flower board shorts, and an assortment of other odds and ends.

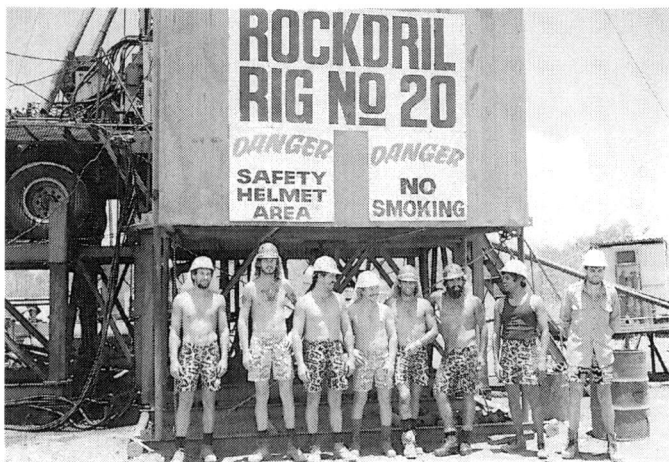

Given that the only personal protective equipment that was mandatory at the time was hardhat and safety boots, everyone dressed up in the loud shorts for work, which looked hilarious up on the drillfloor.

The well, Altree-1, was also being drilled for Pacific Oil and Gas. It was spudded on the 24th September 1988 with the drilling of an 8½ inch pre-collar to 102 m. Upon re-entry of the hole to commence coring operations it was found to be closed off below 64 m and could not be deepened below 75 m as a result of severe caving and lost circulation. The hole was plugged and abandoned on the 2nd October 1988. The rig was skidded 3 m and Altree-2 was spudded on the 5th October 1988 and cored to a total depth of 1699.85 m. The well was drilled in the McArthur Basin and spudded in Cretaceous claystones and sandstones and drilled the Cambrian Tindall Limestone and Nutwood Downs Volcanics prior to intersecting the Proterozoic Roper Group. Poor to fair oil shows were noted and a full suite of wireline logs were run before plugging and abandoning the well on the 10th December 1988.

With the drilling completed the rig and camp were demobilised and transported back to the base in Alice Springs. The crew who weren't needed for the trip to Alice Springs were dropped off at the airport in Katherine from where we would all fly to Darwin and then onto Brisbane. Christopher was now 17 months old and this would be his last hitch out on a rig until he would eventually start working on drilling rigs himself when he finished school at 17½ years of age.

Chapter 6

1989 - 1994

STAY-AT-HOME MOTHER

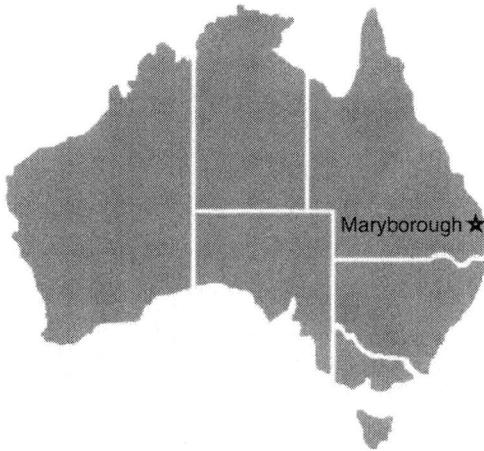

In early 1989 I became pregnant with our second child. While Gary continued to work away for usually 12 weeks at a time, I stayed at home in Maryborough and prepared for the delivery of our second baby. I was scheduled for another cesarean delivery on the 4th October 1989 so Gary arranged to be home a couple of days before. The delivery went to plan and Christopher now had a baby brother, Alexander.

My mother came up from Melbourne to help look after Christopher while I was in hospital and stayed for a couple of weeks while I adjusted to looking after a new born baby and a 2-year old toddler. Within 2 weeks of the cesarean birth Gary went back to work and Mum flew back to Melbourne, leaving me with Christopher and Alex and a new "normal" to adjust to. I actually found it a relief to be on my own with the kids and not have to worry about cooking main meals and fitting into an adult's routine. I was always more relaxed when I was at home by myself and could take advantage of the kids nap times to rest myself.

When Alex was a few months old a gym opened up in Maryborough that had a crèche facility so when they were advertising for staff I applied to work as an aerobics and gym floor instructor.

"The Body Corporate" gym became part of my daily routine and I spent every weekday morning there during the crèche hours of 9 – 11am, instructing in the gym, taking aerobics classes or just doing my own training. It was great getting back into my much-missed aerobics classes and weight training and I made lots of new friends in my adoptive hometown.

Christopher and Alex were well looked after in the crèche and I loved having those 2 hours each day to be childfree and doing what I loved most – and getting paid for it! The staff members were all a great bunch of people and we had a lot of fun together with many of them also having small children. The business changed owners after a few years but the new owners were also great to work for and also had young children of their own.

Happy, motivated staff are at your service . . . the Body Corporate specialises in designing safe, interesting fitness programs.

Gary continued to work away for usually 12 weeks at a time but always managed to time a break around Christopher's birthday in July and Alex's birthday in October. He always had around 4 weeks at home over the Christmas/New Year period as this is the "wet season" up north and drilling programs generally close down over this period due to inaccessible roads after heavy rains.

In 1991 I fell pregnant with our third child. I continued to work and train at the gym right up until the day I went into labour which happened a couple of days before I was scheduled to have a cesarean. Gary was lucky to make it home just in time for the unexpected natural delivery of our daughter Rebecca on the 4th September 1991.

For the next 2 weeks I had Gary and my mum at home with me as I adjusted to looking after three kids under 5 years of age. As soon as they both left I started working and training back at the gym, only now I had 3 kids to drop off at the gym crèche each morning. I quickly adjusted to doing what was necessary to get back into a routine and managed to get the kids fed, bathed and dressed and in the gym by 9am every weekday.

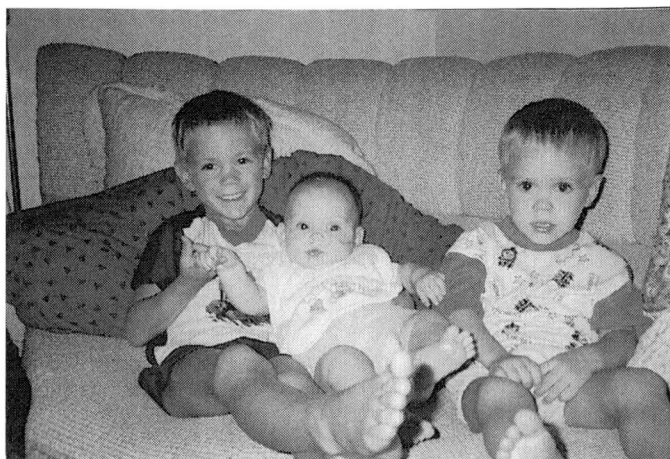

Up until the late 1980's there was no official accreditation for working in the fledgling fitness industry and all you needed was the passion and ability to give it a go. This soon all changed when the marketability of the industry was recognized and it was decided that a formal qualification was needed to make the industry more professional.

This qualification was called the "Fitness Leader" certification and it soon became the benchmark qualification for anyone who wanted to work in the industry. I began a correspondence Fitness Leader course in 1991 when I was pregnant with Becky and then completed the final theory exam in January 1992. As well as the Fitness Leader certification there was the beginning of a registration system for Fitness Leaders, which once achieved, had to be renewed every two years. To be able to renew it you had to (and still do) achieve a certain amount of "Continuing Education Credits" (CEC's), which you do by attending workshops and seminars relating to the industry and your specialties.

With the birth of "Step Reebok" classes in 1989 in the US it wasn't long before it reached the shores – and gyms – of Australia. By 1992 the aerobics phenomenon was a moneymaking machine and instructor courses and workshops were springing up everywhere. In addition to the Fitness Leader qualification there were also specialty courses for aerobics classes, Step Reebok, nutrition, and resistance training – all of which I paid to attend to increase my skills base and also for re-registration purposes.

In 1993 Reebok introduced a new gimmicky class called "Slide Reebok", for which I also became a certified instructor.

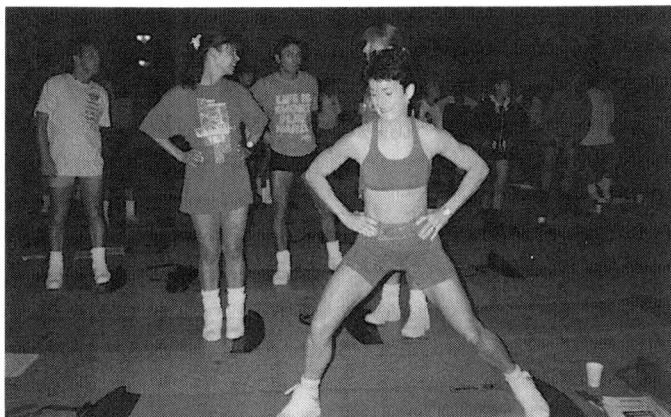

At the start of 1994 Gary received a promotion to an office position as the Operations Manager of Rockdril's growing base in Mount Isa. With the boom of exploration activity in the Mount Isa Proterozoic mineral province Rockdril's activities quickly expanded and Gary took on the office-based position and for the first time in his 14 years with Rockdril he would no longer be working away. He moved up alone at first, while he got established up there, and the kids and I were to follow a few months later. Despite the move to an outback town I was over the moon at being able to live in a mining town where I would feel a bit closer to my professional peers, even if I wasn't still working back as a geologist yet.

The year we made the move Christopher was in Grade 2 and Alex was in pre-school in Maryborough. They were all young enough not to be fazed by the move and we were all excited when it came to make the 1,700 km (1,056 miles) drive to Mount Isa.

Chapter 7

1994 - 1998

RETURN TO MY CAREER

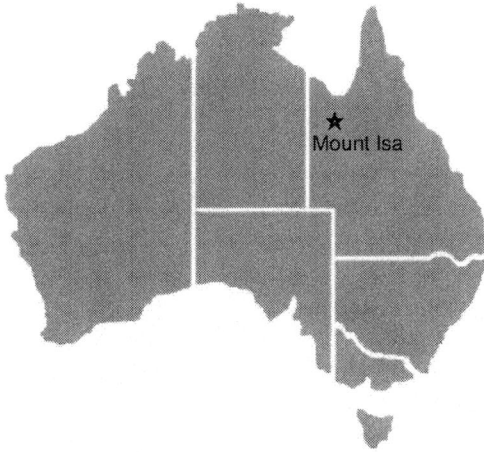

Mount Isa

Mount Isa is the administrative, commercial and industrial centre for Queensland's northwestern region. The city sprung up out of the fields of spinifex after prospector John Campbell Miles stumbled upon one of the world's richest deposits of copper, silver, lead and zinc in 1923. Mount Isa Mines is one of the most productive single mines in world history, and has been continuously mining from underground and open-cut since 1931.

It took us two days to drive to Mount Isa, with a stop

overnight at a hotel in Longreach. We didn't need to take any furniture with us so we were able to carry all our personal items and clothes in a trailer that we towed behind the car.

The drive to northwest Queensland is very boring with near-featureless plains for several hundred kilometres until you reach the edge of the northwest mineral belt, which is characterized by stoney ridges of the outcropping Mount Isa Inlier. The Mount Isa mine and township are hidden in the valley of the Leichhardt River and you don't see them until only a few kilometres out of town when you drive over the crest of a hill and they appear in front of you. The sprawling outback city of around 20,000 people sits in front of the mine site and smelter stacks that dominate the skyline.

Our new home was an old fibro-cement house that sat about 1 metre above the ground on cement pillars. It was on the grounds of the Rockdril yard at Kolongo Crescent, near the Mount Isa airport. Our house was on one side of the large trucking yard and another similar house was on the other side and this would house any Rockdril personnel who were working on getting their rigs ready to go out to a job. In the middle of the yard was a large open-air workshop that the mechanics worked out of.

There was no air-conditioning in the house so the windows and doors were always left open which meant the house was always full of red dust from the trucks driving around the yard.

There was a large hill of stoney outcrop beyond the back fence line and the only vegetation on it was sparsely scattered desert shrubs and spinifex. The entire Mount Isa district is considered spinifex country with hummocky grassland, scattered trees and spikey spinifex being the only vegetation able to survive on the stoney outcrops of the Mount Isa Inlier.

The city experiences mostly a hot semi-arid climate with the summers being very hot, with variable rainfall and humidity owing to the erratic influence of the monsoon. "The Isa" can go for years with having barely any rain but can also have rare wet seasons where tropical monsoonal systems can dump up to a metre of rain between November and March. Summertime maximum temperatures are commonly between 40 - 45°C (103 - 115°F) and the winter daytime maximum generally around 26°C (79°F).

****

Once we were settled in the house and Christopher resumed school after the mid-year holidays, I sought out the local gym and applied for a position as a gym and

73

aerobics instructor. One of my gym instructor friends from Maryborough knew the owner-managers of the gym in Mount Isa and recommended I look them up and it wasn't long before I was working at "The Fitness Warehouse" on Beverley Lane in Mount Isa. They also had a crèche facility for two hours each morning so it wasn't long before I was back into a routine of dropping Christopher off at school and Alex and Becky off at the crèche before training or working in the gym from 9 to 11am every weekday.

In 1994 I received my Nutrition certification and also attended many aerobics workshops in Brisbane. The aerobics scene was such a booming industry by now that the main fitness industry training company "Network for Fitness Professionals" (now known as "Australian Fitness Network") were holding annual fitness conventions at Jupiter's Casino on the Gold Coast in Queensland. These conventions had been running since 1989 and they consisted of three days of non-stop aerobics classes for instructors. I attended my first convention in 1994 and joined hundreds of other lycra-clad instructors in the normally very formal facilities of the Casino-Hotel complex. During this period of time "sport aerobics" was a worldwide competitive sport and Australians featured very strongly on the world stage. World champion competitors were crowd favourite presenters at the conventions and the energy they exuded in the workshops was lapped up by the fitness fanatics. It was always fun going back home after a convention and surprising the class participants with all the new moves you learnt over the three days of instructor training.

Being predominantly a mining town, the population was very transient so the gym was a great place for newcomers to "The Isa" to meet people. Being part of the tight-knitted group of instructors was a fun way to get to know many of the demographically eclectic people of Mount Isa. Despite being a very remote area, sport played a very big role in the social fabric of the city, for children and adults alike. The gym was the focal point of many people's social lives, as well as sporting lives.

In 1995 Alex joined Christopher at school which left only Becky at home all day with me. By now we had moved out of the hot, dusty house at the Rockdril yard and after about one year of living in a rented house in the suburb of Soldiers Hill, we bought our own home on the other side of town at Happy Valley.

Gary's role as the Operations Manager for Rockdril meant he worked closely with many of the geologists working in the area, which meant I finally started to get more contact also with people in the industry. "Wining and Dining" potential clients was the standard way of securing drilling contracts and I generally joined Gary when he met with the geologists over dinner at usually the best restaurant in town at the time – the Verona.

After a meeting with clients one day, Gary came home and said that someone asked if he thought I'd be interested in working at the mine, as they needed someone to log a backlog of core that had built up over time. He didn't know any specifics but I didn't have to wait long before finding out because I got a phone call from the Senior Geologist at the Hilton Mine the very next day asking if I'd be interested in a job out there logging core. She explained how they do "PC logging" and asked if I'd done any before and I wracked my brain trying to figure out what she meant and then panicked when I realized what she meant by "PC" – computers!!! I'd never even used a "PC" and choked back my words as I admitted that I hadn't but to my surprise she didn't seem fazed by my admission and organized a time the next day for me to meet her for an interview.

Hilton Mine (now known as George Fisher South) was a silver, lead and zinc mine, 22 km (14 miles) north of the town based operations of Mount Isa Mines (MIM). The mineralisation was hosted in the same dolomitic Urquhart Shale as the MIM deposit and suspected to have had a similar diagenesis. Geologists working for MIM discovered the deposit in 1947 and it was named after Charlie Hilton who, at the time, was the MIM manager. Metal prices were too low for the original start up planned in 1969 so production didn't start until 1989.

I met up with the senior geologist, Cathy Hooper, out at Hilton Mine and she took me on a tour of the surface operations at the mine and in particular, the coreshed. There was 20,000 metres of core that had been drilled for underground stope delineation that still had to be logged and processed and she was hoping I could be the person to get it done. After showing me through the logging process I mustered all the confidence I could and told her I was up for the job...and she offered it to me!

Becky was 4 years old now and already attending preschool three days a week so I booked her into a childcare centre for the other two days and negotiated with Cathy to work 30 hours a week and planned to work six hours per day Monday to Friday, which meant I could still drop the kids off at school and day care and pick them up again in the afternoon. As my working hours wouldn't divert any of my time from the kids before or after school it was easy for them to adjust to me now having a "full time" job. After being a full time mum for the past eight years I was super excited about working as a geologist again.

I worked for six hours straight, from 9am to 3pm, every weekday. The logging was done directly onto a laptop computer by a computerized core logging system known as "DATCOL". Not only was the logging data entered directly into a laptop but it was entered via a scanning wand and sheet of barcodes, rather than typing on a keyboard. I picked it up pretty quickly and before long I was ploughing my way through the backlog.

The Hilton orebodies lie within the Mount Isa-McArthur Basin system that are part of the Northern Australian Platform cover, which is a 5 to 15 km thick volcano-sedimentary succession. Deposition took place in three super-basins, which represent three nested cycles of deposition and exhumation, with the youngest of these being the Isa super-basin. All of the major stratabound silver-lead-zinc (Ag-Pb-Zn) deposits of the Mount Isa and Hilton Mine system are hosted by the Isa super-basin. The Hilton orebody lies within the Middle Proterozoic (1653 Ma) pyritic, dolomitic siltstone of the approximately 1000 m thick Urquhart Shale within the Western Fold Belt of the Mount Isa Inlier.

At the time I started working at Hilton Mine, MIM had just started a drilling campaign for a feasibility study into the prospectivity of the northern extension of the Hilton deposit which had now been called the George Fisher deposit, 2 km north of the Hilton deposit. Much of the more easily accessible higher-grade ore at Hilton had already been mined and recoveries were becoming increasingly more difficult in the structurally complex southern end of the deposit. *(By 1998 production at Hilton was slowed in favour of the more accessible and higher grades of the George Fisher Mine.).*

A major feature in the thinly laminated stratabound ores of Mount Isa, Hilton and George Fisher were sequences of potash-rich horizons, which were locally termed tuff marker beds (TMB's). Suspected to be of volcaniclastic origin, these TMB's showed a constant relationship to the orebodies and were used in establishing the stratigraphic succession. High importance was placed on identifying TMB's within the mine sequence during core logging operations. Obtaining a positive identification was done by testing suspected TMB's for their reaction to sodium cobaltinitrite after etching with hydrofluoric acid, a procedure that took place under a fume hood given the extreme consequences if this acid was to come into contact with your skin. It was a routine test that was carried out several times a day with just a minimum of PVC gloves and apron worn while performing the test. (*With the introduction of ever-increasing safety standards this testing procedure would eventually be an almost prohibitive exercise*).

Despite the mining industry generally being dominated by males, it was refreshing to be part of an almost all-female geology department where the team leader, senior geologist, and three out of the four mine geologists were females (seen with me in the photo below).

Within the three MIM minesites of the Copper Mine, the Lead Mine and Hilton Mine, there were dozens of geologists employed in the company and it was a very close-knit professional community. There were regular Friday afternoon technical talks where everyone would get together with a guest speaker giving a presentation on an appropriate topic and later having drinks over a BBQ dinner. Despite the transient nature of the professional workforce there was always a strong core of long-term employees who had made Mount Isa their home. Many of them had young families like me, and participated in local sporting events so it was a very social environment in which to work and live. It was a wonderful place to bring up a young family and develop your career with one of the biggest and most progressive mining companies of the time.

Once I began working at Hilton Mine I could no longer attend the gym in the morning but continued to take the odd aerobics class in the evening after work. To maintain my fitness I set up a small gym in our home and got up at 5:30 am every weekday morning and trained in the gym for half an hour then went for a 5 km run around the streets of Mount Isa before showering and getting the

81

kids up and ready for school. On the weekends I'd train with my gym instructor friend Claire either at the Fitness Warehouse gym or at her dad's home gym.

I continued to attend fitness industry workshops and the annual NETWORK Fitness Convention at Jupiter's Casino on the Gold Coast in 1995 and 1996 and maintained my gym and aerobics instructor accreditation and registration. All three of my kids were now attending primary school which was conveniently around the corner from where we lived so they all walked to school, which saved me time before and after work.

By August 1997 I had completed logging the 20,000 metres of core and started helping the mine geologist, Roslyn Budd, interpret the geology of the structurally challenging southern end of the Hilton deposit using cross-sections generated by the diamond drill holes I had logged. I also performed the painstaking task of validating the entire geology database for the mine. Until recently, all logging and assaying data was hand-entered into the database which left a lot of room for error given the incredible amount of data that had to be entered – and generally by administrative staff who were not totally familiar with geological vernacular.

It wasn't long before I had worked myself out of a job at Hilton by early 1998 but fortunately managed to get some more contract work at the Copper Mine logging a small backlog of core that they now had.

The coreshed for the Copper Mine was where all the original core from the very beginning of the mine in the 1920's was stored. No diamond core was ever thrown out so the coreshed was stacked from floor to roof with racks of dusty old trays full of historical diamond core samples. I was in awe of the historical significance of this dilapidated old shed after spending the past 2 years in the state-of-the-art coreshed at Hilton Mine.

Mount Isa Mines Limited (MIM) was established on the 19th January 1924. By 1955, MIM had become the largest mining company in Australia and had weathered technical and financial difficulties and industrial unrest to become Australia's largest single creator of export income.

Along with Kalgoorlie, in the Western Australian goldfields, and Broken Hill, another silver-lead-zinc (Ag-Pb-Zn) mine in far western New South Wales, Mount Isa Mines was where many geologists and mining engineers "cut their teeth" after graduating from university.

The copper ore deposits, like the Hilton and Mount Isa silver-lead-zinc ore bodies, are hosted within the Urquhart Shale. In the Mount Isa mine area, the Mount Isa Group strikes north south and has a persistent westerly dip of 65°. It is around 4000 m in thickness and comprises a sequence of alternating units of dolomitic shale and dolomitic siltstone; with relatively minor conglomerate and sandstone at the base.

The individual copper orebodies are contained entirely within a single large irregular silica-dolomite alteration mass, which lies to the south of and overprints the Ag-Pb-Zn orebodies, but still lie within the Urquhart Shale. There is evidence to suggest that the silica-dolomite and copper ore are substantially younger than the Ag-Pb-Zn ore.

The silica-dolomite mass has a strike length of at least

2600 m, maximum width of 530 m and up-dip extent of near 1000 m. Its boundaries cut across bedding. The main gangue minerals are ferroan dolomite and quartz with locally important talc, chlorite and K-feldspar. The silica-dolomite comprises an early progressive growth of exaggerated dolomite grains and porphyroblastic dolomite replacement forming pseudo-breccias via replacement outwards from fractures. This stage destroys earlier textures. The silica replacement stage results in partial to complete pseudomorphic silica replacement of the dolomitic pre-cursors and preserves pre-existing textures.

The main sulphides are pyrite and chalcopyrite with lessor pyrrhotite and cobaltite. They are predominantly present as replacements forming coarse grained aggregates, pseudo-breccias and discontinuous veinlets. Chalcopyrite deposition is largely controlled by coarsely crystalline dolomite precursors.

Copper is mined at both the Enterprise and X41 underground copper mines in Mount Isa, which comprise the largest network of underground mine development in the world.

I was based in the Copper Mine's X41 office and worked alongside the X41 mine geology team which again, was nearly all female except for one lucky male geologist – and this was long before the catch phrase "Gender Equality" was even heard of!

Just like at Hilton Mine, I was logging stope delineation diamond drillholes that were drilled from underground drives which meant that every drillhole contained intersections of beautiful sulphide mineralisation. I never got sick of looking at these rocks – from the laminated silver-lead-zinc ores of Hilton and the Lead Mine to the massive chalcopyrite in silica dolomite of the copper ore bodies.

****

In 1996 Rockdril was bought out by Century Drilling, which didn't affect Gary's job at all but it meant that for the first time since 1980 he would have a change of employer.

In March of 1998 Gary was advised that he would be getting transferred to a base in the Northern Territory where Century Drilling had bought out a local drilling company called Gaden Drilling, which was based in Batchelor, NT. There was a house supplied for him in Batchelor so we all planned to relocate up there but Gary went up a few months ahead of me and the kids so he could get settled in the new position before we all arrived. It was also best to wait for the mid-year school holidays to give us more time to do the trip up north and move all the kids out of one school and into another. It was sad to be leaving "The Isa" as we had lots of great friends there after our four years living in the town, but it was time to move on. Within days of Christopher celebrating his 11th birthday with his Mount Isa friends on the 1st July 1998 we were all packed up and ready for another long drive even further north from where we already were and into a new state - well, territory to be exact!

Chapter 8

1999 - 2003

OSBORNE MINE, QLD

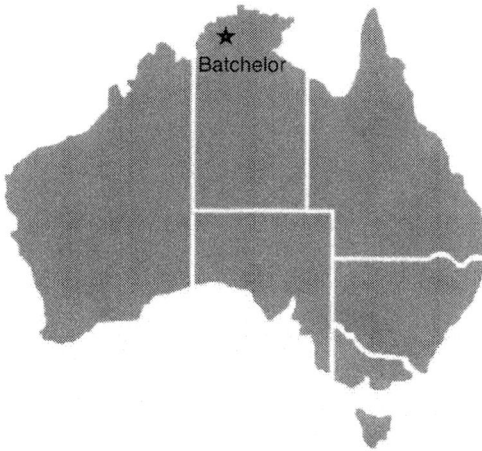

Batchelor

The 1,530 km (950 mile) drive to Batchelor took us two days and it was a pleasant, although quite boring trip. The kids were seasoned long-distance car trippers by now after spending four years in Mount Isa and doing a yearly 2,581 km (1,604 mile) trip to Melbourne to spend Christmas with my family, so this was a relatively "short" drive for us all.

It was always a treat driving along the Stuart and Barkly Highways in the Northern Territory because they were nice wide stretches of straight road that had open speed limits – that is, you could drive as fast as you wanted so long as you weren't driving recklessly. It was the only place in Australia where you could legally do this. The only problem was that you could only safely drive during daylight hours because the kangaroo population was extremely high in these parts of the country and being nocturnal animals, they were attracted to the headlights of the cars at night and appeared out of nowhere from the side of the road. You were pretty well guaranteed of hitting at least one if you dared driving at dawn, dusk or during the night (which I have done – many times!). The Barkly Highway was especially bad for "roos" and cows and while driving during the day you had to watch out for all the "road kill" littering the road that trucks collected during the night. The carcass's would be covered in black crows and wedge tail eagles that would feast on the easy food supply.

You also had to be careful not to collect one of those through your windscreen as you drove over, or around, the road kill as they would stay feasting on the mangled remains until you were almost on top of it. The wedge tail eagles were especially game, as if they were playing a game of "chicken" with you, and the last thing you wanted was to have one of those magnificent, but gigantic-clawed birds-of-prey sitting on your lap in the front seat with you after smashing through your windscreen!

Batchelor is located 98 km (61 mi) south of the Northern Territory's capital city of Darwin and is the gateway to the beautiful Litchfield National Park.

For a small town of only about 400 people it has quite an important historical significance in the remote "Top End" of Australia.

A small civilian aerodrome that was built there in 1933 found itself being substantially upgraded during World War II and became a major base for not only the Royal Australian Air Force but also the United States Army Air Forces in the defense of Australia. It was also used by units of the Royal Netherlands East Indies Army Air Forces.

In 1948 uranium was discovered at Rum Jungle, the area deriving its name from an incident when a thief stole 750 ounces of gold from miners after getting them drunk with rum.

The Australian Government funded the setting up of a mine and treatment plant to provide uranium oxide concentrate to the UK-US Combined Development Agency under a contract which ran from 1953 to 1962. The Australian Atomic Energy Commission was responsible for the mine, although management of it was contracted out to a subsidiary company of the Rio Tinto Group which built the township of Batchelor 8 km south of the mine to accommodate the mining personnel.

Production from the open-cut area started in 1953 and proved to be one of the largest economic influences in the development of the Top End before closure of the mine in 1971.

Gaden Drilling was a small local drilling company that was established in 1976 by Peter Gaden. The company was run out of a yard in Cameron Road, Batchelor, with Peter Gaden also living in the town, on Mardango Crescent. When the company was bought out, both the yard and residential property in Batchelor were now the property of Century Drilling and we were about to set up home in Peter Gaden's old house.

The township of Batchelor was like a little tropical oasis after the long drive through the hot, dry semi-arid desert region of central Australia from Mount Isa. The small town centre boasted beautiful lush, manicured lawns and tropical gardens, which the locals proudly maintained. It had been a past recipient of the "Northern Territory

Tidy Towns" award and the residents had made the effort to keep the town in its award-winning state (*which would find it taking out the Australian Tidy Town Award in 2000*). Having an average annual rainfall of 1,545 mm (61 inches) and warm to hot, humid conditions all year round meant mowing the lawns at our new home was going to be a weekly event!

The house on Mardango Crescent was a lovely, spacious, well maintained home which helped make the adjustment period as painless as possible.

There was only one shop in Batchelor and that was an old-fashioned general store which sold pretty well everything. Prices were quite expensive though, so most people did a weekly shopping trip to Palmerston, which was 80 km north, just before Darwin.

Once the school term started I got the kids enrolled in the Batchelor Area School, which was only a short walk away, down the end of our street. The school catered for students from Transition (Pre-school) to Year 9 although most people sent their high school-aged children to the bigger secondary schools in Darwin.

It was Christopher's third primary school and Alex and Becky's second and although a bit shy to start off with, they settled in easily and made new friends pretty quickly. Although Batchelor was a socially challenged community it seemed a very pleasant, and safe, place to bring up kids.

Once I got the kids settled in their new school I started looking around for a new job. There was quite a bit of mining and exploration being done in the Top End so I was hoping to find something, but after a few months of door-knocking all the company offices in Darwin and surrounding areas I was unable to find anything.

In the meantime, I looked for the nearest gym that held aerobics classes and the closest one to Batchelor was in Humpty Doo, a rural community 67 km north of Batchelor and 40 km southeast of Darwin. I approached the owner/manager at "Rural Results" and asked if they needed any more aerobics instructors and it wasn't long before I was rostered onto the timetable and resumed taking classes.

As well as taking aerobics classes, I had also set up the gym equipment I had brought with us from our home in Mount Isa and continued weight training every day while the kids were at school. In December of 1998 I attended the NETWORK Fitness Convention again but it was now held in Melbourne rather than the Gold Coast. There was also a stronger focus on personal training now, with lots of lecture sessions on specialty disciplines like nutrition, weight training, alternative therapies and many others. It was no longer a three day "aerobics fest", in fact the classes were no longer even called "aerobics" classes and had since been remarketed as "group fitness" classes.

Personal training was just starting to become more mainstream after starting out as something that only Hollywood stars could afford to do. Although it would still take several years before it would become a more accepted and affordable way of getting fit, the progressive change from being just a gym or aerobics instructor to a personal trainer created a whole "sea change" in the industry.

****

In January of 1999 I received a phone call out of the blue from a senior mine geologist at Osborne Mine in north west Queensland, asking if I was interested in a job at the mine. They had a backlog of stope delineation diamond core that needed to be logged and they had heard that I was the best person for the job! To my surprise, I was to learn that one of the mine geologists at Osborne had previous worked at Hilton and knew my friend Roslyn Budd who gave them my contact details when she heard they needed a contract geologist.

When I first spoke on the phone I couldn't really see how I could possibly take on the role when I lived in the Northern Territory, but the geologist explained how Osborne was a "fly in-fly out" minesite and everyone was flown to the site from Townsville on chartered mine flights. After getting a brief explanation of what was involved I told him I'd call him back after discussing it with Gary. Gary said, "Go for it!" so I rang the Osborne Mines geology team leader back and discussed my day rate and roster. I was told I'd have to pay for my own flights from Darwin to Townsville but I managed to negotiate an increase in the day rate to compensate for that. I would be working a 14/7 roster, which meant I would be working onsite for 14 days and then have 7 days break, of which two days would be spent travelling to and from home.

After a few phone calls the deal was done and I received an official Offer of Employment letter with a start date of the 3rd February, 1999, which meant I had to fly from Darwin to Townsville on the 2nd February in time to catch the chartered flight out to the minesite from

Townsville the next morning.

This job opportunity, gained through word-of-mouth by a friend of a friend, taught me my most valuable lesson about working as a contractor in this industry — "never burn your bridges". Having respect from your peers is the most important tool in a contractors toolbox — it gives you the ability to have a strong network looking out for you and a good reputation is a powerful negotiating tool when you came to securing your next role.

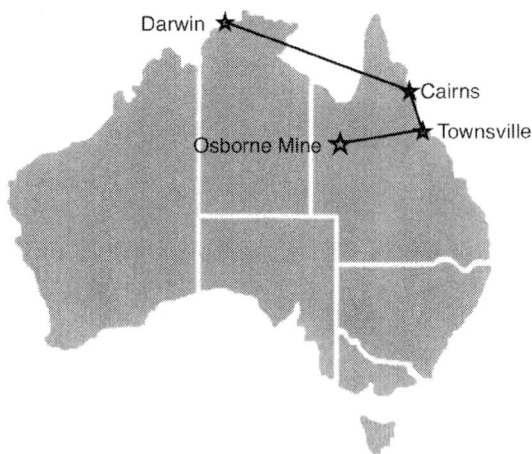

While I was extremely excited to be starting a new job, the timing of it was less than ideal. The day I had to leave for my first hitch just happened to be the first day back at school for the kids *and* they would all be starting at a new school in Humpty Doo.

By the end of 1998 I had decided to enroll the kids back into the Catholic school system, which would have them attending the Catholic primary school in Humpty Doo starting from February in 1999. This would be

Christopher's last year of primary school in Year 7 and Alex would be in Year 4 and Becky in Year 2.

There were quite a few kids from Batchelor going to the school already and there was a bus that picked them up on the Stuart Highway and took them to the school, but they had to be dropped off and picked up from this bus stop each day, which was about a 20-minute drive from Batchelor.

Being their first day at a new school I drove them all the way to the school and saw them get settled in their new classes before leaving for the airport to fly to Townsville. The boys stoically put on a brave face but poor Becky was very upset when it came time for me to leave and she put up quite a struggle, with the school principal doing a fantastic job of freeing her vice-like grip from my arms and reassuring her she would be fine. It was very distressing for both of us but I was determined to give it a go, knowing that if it became too difficult to manage the lifestyle change with the kids then I could always give it up and stay at home.

There was no direct flight from Darwin to Townsville so I had to go via Cairns with a several hour stopover there. When I got to Cairns airport I went to the airline lounge and sent a fax to the school addressed to Becky and told her how much I loved her, then rang the school and asked if they could take the fax to Becky in her classroom. It was all I could do at the time to try and cheer her up and I hoped it would help ease her anxiety and distress even just a little bit.

I had some friends living in Townsville and one of them was Annie, an aerobics-instructor friend from my time spent living in Mount Isa. Annie picked me up when I arrived at Townsville airport and I stayed at her place. It was great being able to catch up with her now every couple of weeks on my way to and from work.

****

Until recent years, workers in remote mining operations in Australia resided in townships that were developed by the resource companies near the site of the mine, but in the early 1980's mining companies began to adopt the use of Fly In-Fly Out (FIFO) work practices as an alternative to purpose-built townships. Developments in communications and transportation resulted in FIFO work practices becoming a viable option.

The move away from purpose-built company towns gained momentum as the costs involved in constructing and maintaining towns increased and the costs associated with closing down towns once the resource was exhausted or economically unviable became unworkable. Additionally, a tight labour market, skilled labour shortages and the worker preference for their families to live in metropolitan areas rather than rural areas with limited services and opportunities, also contributed to the rise in popularity of working FIFO.

FIFO mining operations, by definition, are those, which involve work in relatively remote locations where food and lodging accommodation is provided for workers at the work site, but not for their families. Employees spend a fixed number of days working 12-hour shifts at the site, followed by a fixed number of days at home.

****

Osborne Mine was a copper-gold mine located 195 km (121 miles) south east of Mount Isa in northwest Queensland. At the time of my arrival in 1999 it was owned and operated by Placer Dome Inc. but it would see a succession of new owners with Barrick Gold Corp acquiring it in 2006 and then Chirnova Resources taking over operations in 2010 before the final mine closure in 2015. Production began in 1995 with open-pit mining operations and this was replaced with underground operations in 1996.

The Osborne orebody was based on an ironstone-hosted replacement-type copper gold mineralisation and had a complex deformation and metamorphism history. It was hosted within the Eastern Fold Belt sub province of the more extensive Mount Isa Mineral Province. The two main orebodies extended below 600 metres from surface with a third zone to the east forming a high-grade pod about 200 metres below surface. Chalcopyrite was the primary copper mineral, occurring as very coarse grains associated with replacement and brecciation textures, commonly in zones of silicification. Average grades were about 2% copper and 1 gram per tonne of gold with native gold being very rare.

The roster for most people working at Osborne was 14 days on and 7 days off with most people residing in Townsville, so their commute to work was about a 90-minute flight via the chartered mine flights. I lined up at the Osborne Mine check-in counter at Townsville airport with the other mine workers, with a bag containing enough toiletries for 2 weeks, and a pair of steel-capped boots – all other work clothes would be supplied once I arrived on site.

Once everyone was checked in we were all led in single file along the tarmac to the Metroliner that would be taking us on the 950 km flight to the mine site. The 19-seat twin-turboprop plane reminded me of a pencil with wings and I was grateful for my small stature when I took my seat in the narrow fuselage. I was the only person who didn't have to crouch down while walking to their seat. The seats were stripped down versions of a normal airline seat and I felt sorry for all the bigger people on the plane having to suffer the next 90 minutes in such cramped conditions.

After about 90 minutes of flying over the mostly boring semi-arid, flat landscape of north Queensland we finally started the descent into Osborne Mine with views of the isolated accommodation village and mine site appearing like foreign objects on a lunar landscape. It was obvious just looking out the window that this inhospitable landscape would have an equally harsh climate and I wasn't surprised to walk down the small folded-down steps leading from the plane to the bitumen tarmac and be greeted by the outback summertime searing heat. It was only 9am but already the temperature would have been over 30°C (86°F), and the flies started swarming as soon as you left the air-conditioned cabin of the plane.

It had been several years since I'd lived in such remote isolation but the 4 years spent living in Mount Isa had hardened me to the harsh climate so I wasn't concerned about that. But you never get used to the flies.

There was a bus waiting for us at the airport and after grabbing our bags off the plane we boarded the bus and drove the few kilometres to the accommodation village, where a member of the HR department would meet me. The somber faces of the incoming crew on the bus would soon be replaced with the excited outgoing crew, many of whom already had a beer in their hand after knocking off from night shift only a few hours before. Being a "wet mess" (dining area that serves alcohol) the bar was the meeting point for everyone waiting for the arrival of the bus that would be the start of their journey home for a week of R & R. I was soon to learn that there is no better feeling than the anticipation felt while waiting for the plane to land on fly-out day!

After being met by the Human Resources lady I followed her down the concrete path that led from the Mess to the accommodation cabins to where my room would be. The camp housed about 180 employees in individual cabins that had four fully self-contained rooms per cabin. Each room had its own little verandah and inside the room there was a wardrobe, study desk and single bed and a small ensuite bathroom. It was luxurious compared to the old "dongas" we lived in at the Rockdril camps.

With everyone having their own room most people decorated the walls with posters or family photos and brought a TV out to use with satellite TV channels being provided. When I first arrived there was even a soft porn channel – not that I ever watched it! With everyone being on the minesite for 8 months of the year it made sense to make your room as comfortable as possible because you spent more time sleeping here than you did at home.

The camp had fantastic facilities with a 25-metre swimming pool, tennis court, outdoor cricket nets and a gym. The buffet meals were usually pretty good and the bar area also had a pool table, table tennis table and darts board.

After the tour of the camp and dropping my gear off in

my room, I changed into a set of the khaki work clothes that had been provided, and my steel-capped boots, and left for the drive to the minesite.

It was about a 5 km drive along a bitumen-sealed road to the minesite from the accommodation and the workers generally got driven there in the mine buses. While driving out on that first day I had already decided I would never be catching the bus and would instead walk to work along the road.

After the usual minesite general inductions I got to work on logging the backlog of diamond core that was stacked all around the coreshed. Before long this was cleared and the underground drilling program was ramped up with up to four rigs drilling stope delineation drilling at one stage and near-mine exploration surface drilling also being logged and processed in the minesite coreshed. The geology team in the coreshed would eventually expand to include several graduate geologists logging core on a contract basis with me overseeing the drilling programs for both underground and surface exploration. The core was assayed at the onsite laboratory with routine blanks and standards being included, as per regulatory requirements. The assay results, along with the drillhole logging and survey data, were entered into the mine's database through an "acQuire" data management system.

Everyone worked a 12-hour day, from 6am to 6pm, for 14 days straight so there wasn't a great deal of time to take advantage of the recreational facilities at the camp. I managed to maintain a pretty good fitness regime by walking the 5 km to work along the road each morning and jogging back in the evenings along a dirt track that wound through the bush between the camp and the minesite. Once I got to the camp I'd spend about half an hour in the gym before going for a meal and then heading back to my room for the night.

It was always a good idea to remain vigilant whenever walking around the camp or the minesite because snakes were extremely prevalent and active most of the year, although the summer months were when they were most active. Death adders were the most common snake seen, and as their name suggests, they are one of the most venomous snakes in Australia and globally. They have a broad flattened, triangular head and a thick-banded body, which is a master of camouflage, and its colours vary according to its habitat.

The death adders at Osborne were orange and brown, colours that matched the desert soil and leaf litter, so it was very hard to spot them as they lay coiled in ambush waiting for prey to stumble upon them. Although death adders possess the longest fangs of any Australian snake, they are generally not a threat to humans as they aren't aggressive so they generally won't bother you unless you accidentally stand on one.

Another common snake found around the area was the black-headed python and I came across one of these as I was throwing my washing in the dryer in the laundry one night. It was lying in the gap between two of the machines with its head up off the ground in a striking pose. It scared the daylights out of me and I backed away gingerly as I had no idea at the time that it was a harmless snake. I raced over to my room and rang the mine security guy and he came out and took one look at it and declared it to be a black-headed python and that it was totally harmless. Better to be safe than sorry, I reckon!

I saw many other varieties of snakes in my time at Osborne, including the venomous orange naped snake and also a western taipan, which is considered the most venomous snake in the world. However it is usually quite a shy and reclusive snake, with a placid disposition and prefers to escape from trouble rather than stay and attack. I always made sure I walked with a headlamp when in the dark before and after work, and kept my eyes peeled to the ground. I also carried a pressure bandage with me at all times in the event of sustaining a bite, and hope that someone would come across me on the track sooner rather than later.

As well as having the odd death adder in the coreshed, we also had a few resident goannas (monitor lizards) that sauntered around the core racks and trays. They seemed oblivious to all the noise and activity going on and were clearly comfortable co-habitating with the coreshed crew.

The reptiles were the fun wildlife that we had to live with, not nearly as much fun were the flies. One year they were so bad everyone had to wear fly nets on their head to prevent swallowing flies every time you opened your mouth to talk. Worse still, you would invariably get the occasional fly getting trapped inside the fly net and buzzing frantically against your face, tickling you to death!

****

The kids adjusted to me being away and by the middle of 1999 we had bought a house up in Humpty Doo so we were closer to the school and the amenities of Darwin. I continued working the 14/7 roster for about two years but by then Gary had quit his job with Century Drilling and had also started working away again. Now it became really hard to manage the kids and if Gary and I were both away at the same time we paid a friend to stay in our home and look after the kids for us. I considered quitting my job but first of all tried to see if I could make a compromise so I asked my boss if I could change to a 14/14 roster so I was having 2 weeks off each break and home twice as much as I had been. This meant a drop in pay per month but made it much easier to manage things at home and spend more quality time with the kids.

At the time, we had quite a big team of geologists working in the coreshed so my boss said that if I could work out a roster that suited me but still got all the work done then he was happy, so we managed to work around it by everyone else helping out with the supervising role while I was off site. We had a great geology team and everyone got along really well, including the drilling crews, who we often had Friday night BBQ's with in the contractor's camp.

Just like in Mount Isa, there was a healthy representation of females in the geology department, and even one in the engineering department!

****

When I first started working at Osborne I was flying from Darwin to Townsville with Ansett Airlines, and even paid $350 to join the Golden Wing Club so I could use the airline lounge during my long stopover in Cairns on the way to work. I never had any problems with flight delays or missed flights until September in 2001.

On one of my trips back to work I was wondering why flight crew were having their photos taken while sitting on the rim of the engine of an Ansett plane on the tarmac at Cairns Airport while I was boarding my flight. I assumed it was just a fun thing they decided to do at the time, not realizing that this was going to be the last Ansett flight I would ever take.

On the 12th September 2001, the Ansett group of companies went into voluntary administration. In the early hours of the 14th September, the administrator determined that Ansett wasn't viable to continue and grounded the fleets of Ansett and its subsidiaries. With the flights already in the air at the time the decision was made for them to continue on to their destinations, with most unaware of the devastating news that would greet them at the other end. Customers and few employees had any warning of the stoppage in operations. Everyone had been told in the days leading up to the 14th September that flights would continue on schedule, and most Ansett employees did not find out until they showed up for work at dawn that day. Thousands of passengers were left stranded and more than 16,000 people found themselves out of a job, making it the largest mass job loss event in Australian history.

The grounding of the fleet meant that I no longer had

flights home at the end of my hitch so I had to figure out how to get back to Darwin from the middle of nowhere. With a bit of ringing around I was able to organize a lift in the freight truck that brought supplies out to the minesite from Mount Isa and travelled the 195 km (121 mi) back to the Isa in the truck. Once in Mount Isa I managed to hire a rental car and drove the 1,600 km (994 mi) back to Darwin.

Two weeks later when it was time to return to work, it was practically impossible to get a flight, let alone one I could afford. With Qantas having to pick up the slack from all the flights that had been cancelled, they were having a tough time keeping up with the demand. I decided it was cheaper and more reliable for me to drive my own car to work for the next hitch and wait for things to settle down, and for the backlog of passengers to clear so fares would be a bit cheaper again.

The 1,795 km (1,115 mi) road trip was very uneventful and I was very glad to get to the minesite after the long drive. I only wish the same could be said for the return trip two weeks later.

On my "fly out" day I finished work mid-afternoon and started the drive home. I arrived in Mount Isa after about 2½ hours and stopped to fuel the car up and grab some snacks for the long trip ahead of me. It was getting close to sunset and I wouldn't normally drive at night on these outback roads because of the kangaroos, but I just wanted to get home as quickly as I could so decided to continue driving until I got tired and then just rest on the side of the road for a sleep.

Not long after leaving Mount Isa I started seeing

smoke off in the distance ahead of me and soon realized there were scrub fires on both sides of the road. As I got closer I could see firefighting personnel attending to it and they were allowing the cars to continue through the clouds of smoke that were now choking the stretch of bitumen from both sides. The fires continued for a few kilometres and I slowed down to below 80 km/hour as I was fully expecting to encounter lots of wildlife that would inevitably be racing across the road frantically trying to escape the flames and smoke from their natural habitat.

No matter how alert you are, there's always some dumb kangaroo that jumps out from the side of the road and heads straight into your oncoming car. Usually you have two choices if you happen to see it in time – you can either keep driving and just hope it doesn't do much damage or you can swerve to try and avoid it and in the process run off the side of the road and risk serious damage to both you and your car. Or worse still, you could swerve into an oncoming car travelling in the opposite direction, and that can be *really* bad news.

But this time I didn't have any choice because I didn't even see it come out of the smoke and leap straight into the front left corner of my car. As I inhaled a quick gasp in horror, the 'roo bounced off the wheel guard and disappeared out of sight as I quickly pulled off to the side of the highway to inspect the damage. From the thump it made when it hit I was expecting the worst, and thoughts of being stranded on the Barkly Highway all night flashed through my mind as I anticipated the damage that was probably done. Fully expecting to see a smashed headlight and caved-in wheel arch rubbing against my tyre, I was overwhelmingly surprised to see there was no damage that would prevent me from continuing my drive. While the headlight perspex cover was smashed, it hadn't broken the light itself and the headlight was still brightly shining up at me, and while the wheel arch was bent it wasn't rubbing on the tyre so this wasn't going to pose a problem either. Phew! I couldn't believe my luck, and after taking a few deep breathes and a huge sigh of relief, I jumped back in the car and continued on my way.

After stopping to stretch my legs and getting something to eat at Camooweal just before the Northern Territory border, I continued driving into the night until I got to the Barkly Homestead. It was very frustrating having to keep my speed down on such a flat stretch of road along the Barkly Tablelands but I couldn't risk hitting any more rogue 'roos. I filled up the car with fuel and freshened up in the bathroom of the roadhouse then crashed on the back seat of my car for the night.

After waking at about 5am I slid into the drivers seat and made a start on the 1,150 kilometres I still had to drive to get home. I cautiously sat on 80 km/hour as the morning twilight welcomed in the new day, and concentrated on watching not only for any live kangaroos wanting to head-butt my car again, but also for all the road-kill that was littering the highway after the trucks had irreverently mowed them down overnight. There were not only dead kangaroos but also dead cattle, both of which were too big to drive over, so you had to swerve around them to avoid damaging your car.

There were barely any other cars on the road and I was chilled out listening to music when all of a sudden another bloody roo jumped out from the left side of the road and collided with the middle of the front of my car, rolled up over the windscreen, bounced along the roof and slid off the back of the car. Holy shit that woke me up! My heart was thumping out of my chest as I quickly pulled over on the side of the road and braced myself for the damage I was expecting to see on the front of my car. The engine was still running OK so I left it on while I got out of the car – too scared to turn it off in case it wouldn't start again. The roo was huge and it hit dead centre of the bonnet so I was sure the whole front of my car would have been stoved in – which it was. I didn't want to lift the bonnet up to check for damage under it because I suspected that I wouldn't have been able to close it again if I had. I checked underneath for any leaking fuel, water or hydraulic fluid but there wasn't any, and the engine was purring away quietly as it should, so I decided to start driving again, albeit extremely slowly, and check for any warning lights or engine noises as I continued the drive. I gradually increased my speed up to 80 km/hour again and after a few minutes of trouble-free driving I whooped in excitement at the fact I had dodged my second "roo bullet" of the drive and was continuing my homeward-bound journey.

I was extremely relieved to see daylight again because it meant the kangaroos were no longer such a dangerous threat. I slowly let my guard down somewhat and relaxed enough to start enjoying the music and the peacefulness of the long, lonely stretch of remote highway.

The Barkly and Stuart Highways both still had unrestricted speed limits at this stage so the small amount of traffic that you did come across was generally moving very fast. When you're sitting on 130 km/hour and a three-trailer road train passes you in the opposite direction travelling at the same speed, then you can expect your windscreen to get hit by some very fast-moving stones that get kicked up off the road. With the force and sound of a bullet, I collected a stone in the middle of the windscreen and the force of it instantly created a menacing-looking star that I knew would only get bigger as I continued to drive. And continue to drive I did. When I got to Katherine and had mobile phone coverage, I stopped and rang Gary, who was home on break, and let him know I was only about 3 hours away and that I'd sustained a "bit" of damage on the trip. When I finally rolled into the carport at home, Gary was waiting for me and rolled his eyes and shook his head when he saw the front of my car as I came to a stop and shut down the engine. We both stood there for a few minutes, amazed at the dilapidated state of the car and the fact that it still kept driving and got me home. I decided to fly to work after that – no matter how expensive the flights were. Lesson learnt.

****

While working at Osborne I continued to take aerobics classes at the gym in Humpty Doo when I was home on break. Les Mills pre-choreographed classes were now becoming very popular and a Les Mills trainer came up from Sydney to do a training course for Darwin instructors in March of 2000 so I attended it, along with the other instructors from Rural Results, to obtain my "Body Combat" certification. In June of 2001 I attended another fitness industry convention at Darling Harbour in Sydney.

As well as catching up with some old gym friends from Maryborough, it was great to attend workshops and seminars to get up-to-date on the latest industry trends.

I had a fairly well-equipped home gym set up on our back verandah at home and trained every day while the kids were at school, as well as doing 5 km runs down the road we lived on. The only days I didn't do any sort of training were my travel days to and from the minesite.

****

My original contract for the job at Osborne was only for six months but it was continually renewed at the end of every six-month period. After being there for four years I was starting to get itchy feet. I still loved the job and the great team I worked with but I felt I needed a change of scenery. Although I'd been a "hard rock" geologist for my entire career and only worked as a geologist in the mineral industry, I had a yearning to get involved with the offshore oil and gas industry and broaden my horizons. The experience living in the drilling camps with Gary when he was drilling slim-hole oil and gas wells had given me a taste of what was involved and I wanted to explore it further.

I knew the entry-level job for geologists in the oil and gas industry was generally as a "mudlogger" and with my six years of experience in core logging, drilling program supervision and data collection I figured I'd be more than capable of taking on the role.

There were four major companies supplying mudlogging services to the offshore industry at the time so I hunted online for contact details for them all and sent my resume to the human resources departments of all the companies, with an explanation of my desire to work offshore. After a couple of months the only responses I received were that they had received my resume and would keep it on their files should a position come up. With such a lack-lustre response I realized the HR department route was not going to be best way to secure a job so I needed to be more resourceful. I recognized the need to get more "personal" with the people who were actually in charge of the muddlogging jobs in these companies and contact them directly, rather than going through the HR departments. Over the next couple of months I managed to track down some names of supervisors with some of the companies and I emailed them directly and sent them my resume, explaining how I wanted to get a start working offshore. But I still didn't get much of a response beyond being told my resume would be kept on file for future reference. I was starting to believe what everyone was telling me about the offshore oil and gas industry – "you needed to know someone to get in" – but I didn't know anyone so it was starting to look like I needed to be even more resourceful in my attempts to get a foot in the door.

With three of the four companies being based in Perth, I decided to fly there at my own expense and meet with these people face-to-face as I knew it would be harder to give a knock-back in person than by email. I emailed the contacts I had for each company and explained that I was going to be in Perth on a particular day and asked if I could organize to have an interview with the operations managers while I was there. One didn't reply at all while the other two replied but didn't really commit to anything. I didn't take this as a knock-back but rather a challenge to do all I could to make them want to employ me once they had met me.

During my next two-week break from work I flew to Perth and went to the head offices of two of the companies I had been in contact with. After talking to the field manager at the first company I was told I could have a job, starting pretty well straight away, but the day rate was so low I had to hold back from showing my surprise – and disgust – at what he was offering me. I knew it was going to be a backward step pay-wise from what I was getting as a supervisor at Osborne but this wasn't even worth thinking about. I left feeling a bit disappointed if this was what I could expect to be paid working offshore, but I still had another company I wanted to visit so I continued on my mission.

The second company I visited was Sperry Sun (Halliburton) and after rocking up at the reception desk I asked if I could speak to the manager who I had been in email contact with. I didn't have any prior appointment, which was a problem for the receptionist, but I was insistent and explained how I was only in Perth for the day and wanted to see the person while I was there. She explained that he was out for lunch so I asked what time he would be back and told her I would come back then. Which I did. Eventually they realized I wasn't going to leave until someone interviewed me so they got not just one person, but also a team of their field supervisors, and interviewed me for a possible position working offshore. At the end of the interview they said they would have a position coming up in a couple of months and I was happy to hear the day rate I could expect to start on was considerably more than what the other company had offered me so I told them I'd love to take the position once it became available. I flew back to Darwin that evening feeling pretty confident I had accomplished my mission on my brief trip to Perth.

****

I continued working at Osborne and decided not to say anything about my plans to leave until I got a definite start date for working offshore. And it was just as well I did because it was another couple of months before I finally got an email from Sperry Sun saying an offshore job was starting up that they planned to put me on.

It was hard giving notice of my resignation because I was part of a fantastic team at Osborne and after 4½ years at the minesite I had made lots of great friends. The years I was working at Osborne saw the price of gold drop to under $400 an ounce, 30 year low prices, which threatened to close the operations at Osborne but it managed to just stay afloat with the help of the contribution its copper production made. One of the highlights of my time at Osborne was watching the gold bars getting poured. It was like a covert operation and you had to get special permission and clearance checks done before you were allowed to witness it, which all added to the excitement.

But now it was time to leave and embark on a totally new direction in my career, which was both scary and exciting at the same time. I'd managed to make the first step of crossing over from the minerals industry to oil and gas, so now I just had to jump in with both feet and give it my best shot!

117

Chapter 9

2003

NORTH WEST SHELF, WA

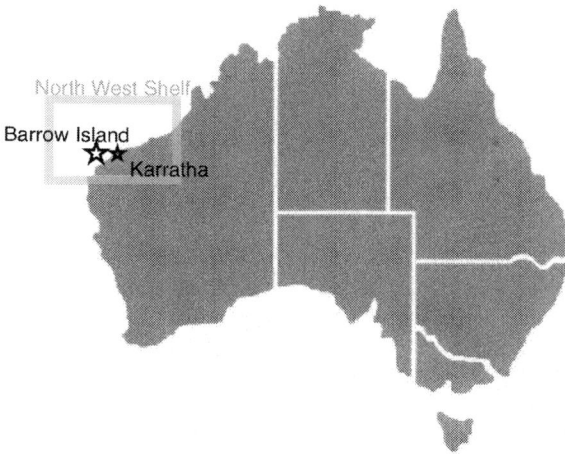

In July of 2003 I flew to Perth to undertake the training I would need to be able to work offshore. Due to the need to fly on helicopters over the water, it's mandatory for everyone working on the North West Shelf in Western Australia to complete the Tropical Basic Offshore Safety Induction and Emergency Training course (TBOSIET). The two-day course covers offshore facility abandonment and sea survival procedures, response to fire incidents, first aid and helicopter underwater escape training (HUET).

I was excited to be doing the training but I soon realized the HUET wasn't something to look forward to. It involved being strapped into a module that simulates the interior of a helicopter. The module is submerged under water and rotated until it is upside down while you are still strapped to your seat with a three-point harness. Once the rotating movement of the module stops you have to release your harness - while you're upside down - then push out the closest window and swim through the opening and up to the surface of the pool. While it didn't sound too harrowing at first, it was a totally different story once the water started creeping up my legs to my waist and then getting closer and closer to my face before having to take a deep breathe, and timing it so you did it before the water got to your mouth but not too soon that you'd run out of breathe before you had a chance to escape. Panic sets in as you sit harnessed into your seat and feel powerless against the incoming rush of cold water.

There are very few people who actually enjoy doing their HUET and unfortunately it has to be renewed every four years. It's not uncommon for people to freak out at this part of the course and end up never working offshore. This happened to someone during our course and the instructors offered the person to come back the next day and spend one-on-one time with them so they could overcome their fears – I don't know if they ever did.

With the TBOSIET done and dusted it was time to spend a few days in the Sperry Sun Perth office doing muddlogging training. I worked through a series of training modules on the computer over a few days and then I was deemed ready to go offshore.

My first job was a 4-week hitch on the Ensco 53 for a series of wells being drilled by Apache on the North West Shelf, offshore Western Australia.

The North West Shelf Venture is Australia's largest resource development involving extraction of oil, natural gas and condensate at offshore production platforms, which is piped via seabed pipelines to processing facilities on the mainland. The gas is then exported as liquefied natural gas (LNG) or used domestically as natural gas.

The hydrocarbon reservoirs are contained within the sediments of the Carnarvon Basin, which encompasses over 1,000 km of the west and northwest coast of Western Australia. The onshore part of the basin covers about 115,000 km^2 and the offshore part covers approximately 535,000 km^2 with water depths of up to 3,500 metres. Almost all the hydrocarbon resources are reservoired within the Upper Triassic, Jurassic and Lower Cretaceous sandstones beneath the regional Early Cretaceous seal.

The rig was drilling offshore from Karratha and we flew directly to Barrow Island on a chartered fixed wing flight from Perth domestic airport. From what I could see as we came in to land, Barrow was a flat, arid island covered in spinifex and nothing much else. It looked pretty inhospitable, not at all what you'd expect of an island off the beautiful Western Australian coastline.

We were led off the plane and into the terminal building where we had to sit through the helicopter pre-flight safety briefing, which has to be viewed before every flight to, or from, the rig. The briefing reviews all the safety features of the particular chopper you'll be travelling in and also revises some of the important parts of the HUET course so you know what to do in the event of the aircraft crash-landing into the water. After doing the training course in Perth I was hoping I never had to experience a real live "ditching" of a chopper.

Everyone was provided with a life jacket and headphones that had to be worn at all times while flying offshore. The engine noise is so loud inside the chopper it's essential to also wear earplugs under the headphones, which means you can forget about having any sort of conversation during the flight to the rig.

The flight only took about half an hour, and despite the cramped, uncomfortable noisy conditions, I was pretty excited about my first ever trip to an offshore oilrig.

After landing on the rig everyone was ushered into the briefing room where we were briefed on the current operations. The key personnel in charge of operations were introduced and then everyone who had already worked on the rig before went straight to work, or the newbies like me stayed for a full rig induction. On offshore facilities there is no overlap of personnel at crew change time. The outgoing crews depart on the same chopper their relief arrives on so you only have time to do a quick handover in the time it takes to swap the lifejacket over and the bags get offloaded and outgoing ones get loaded onto the chopper. The chopper doesn't shut down its engines while on the helideck and takes off again as soon as the departing crew are on board.

After having the guided tour around the rig and told all the do's and don'ts, it was time to make my way to the logging unit, meet the Sperry crew and get to work. I was on the "midday to midnight" shift so had to hit the ground running and start working straight away.

The muddlogging unit was the room from where all the

drilling operations were monitored. It was nothing more than a windowless shipping container from the outside, but on the inside it was a fully-equipped, pressurized control room housing up to 6 people at a time, working 12-hour shifts.

As the mudlogger, it was my job to collect the samples that were drilled as they arrived on the surface over the shale-shakers. The drilled rock cuttings come up in slurry of drilling fluid, which is simply referred to as "the mud". The mud is a brew of chemicals in either a water-based or oil-based solution and is pumped down the hole to be used not only as a lubricant for the bit, but also as a medium to lift the cuttings to surface. The properties of the mud are crucial to the successful drilling of a well and are monitored at all times throughout the drilling operations.

Once the cuttings are collected they have to be washed free of the drilling mud and bagged for later investigation and also a small sample is collected on a tray and taken to the muddlogging unit and inspected under a microscope by both the mudlogger and wellsite geologist. A description of the rock is entered into a computer database system and then a graphical report printed at the end of each 24-hour drilling period.

The shifts were mind-numbingly hectic when drilling ahead and I had days when I wondered what the hell I was doing out there. There was so much to learn on the fly that I was often over-whelmed and struggled to cope. Fortunately the wellsite geologist I was on shift with, Peter Gibson, was extremely helpful and patiently taught me how to describe samples, the most frustrating part of the job when "under the pump".

****

Ensco 53 was a small "jack-up" rig, which meant it had three legs that sat on the seabed and the rig was jacked up above the sea level on these legs. It was built in 1982 and looked like it had had a hard life. I shared a 4-man room with three other Sperry ladies who also worked out of the muddlogging unit. There was a set of bunks on each side of the room with curtains that you could pull around the bed to block out any light in the room while you were trying to sleep. With everyone working different shifts there were always people coming and going from the room while you were trying to sleep. We shared a bathroom with another 4-man room – which actually did have "men", not women in it so you had to be careful you locked the bathroom doors whenever you were in there.

There were three levels of accommodation and unfortunately we were on the bottom level and right over the top of the pump room so it was extremely noisy. Earplugs were essential to be able to sleep through all the noise. With my earplugs in and the curtains drawn I managed to sleep pretty well, although I was so exhausted at the end of the 12-hour shifts I don't think any amount of noise would have kept me from falling into a deep sleep. I was used to working 12-hour shifts from my previous minesite jobs but never under such hectically busy conditions.

Unfortunately the old "rust-bucket" of a rig didn't have a gym, except for a home-made bench-press station out in the weather under the helideck, so I stayed content with just running around the helideck in the morning before I started my shift. It was actually pretty nice up there and the migrating whales breaching off in the distance always provided quite a spectacle that kept me entertained while running. You never got sick of watching the majestic mammals and whenever there were sightings it would be announced over the PA system so everyone could watch out for them.

The sub-tropical waters off the northwest coast of Western Australia were teaming with marine life. As well as the humpback whales, there were sharks, turtles and even red-and-white striped sea snakes that would occasionally skim along the surface of the water then dive into the depths out of sight. As if the marine life wasn't interesting enough, there was also a submarine that surfaced right next to the rig one day. It sat above the water level for about half an hour while everyone watched it in amazement. It was all black with no markings so we could only hope that it was an Australian Navy submarine and not an enemy one.

Being a jack-up rig presented some unique challenges in regards to potential hazards. One of them is the possibility of one or more of the legs punching through the seabed when it is jacked up. To lessen the possibility of this happening, a preload test is done before jacking up the rig above the water level. Each leg is loaded incrementally and the load maintained for a certain period of time to make sure the seabed is strong enough to withstand the weight of the rig once it's jacked up above the surface of the water. If underlying strata beneath the seabed are weak then the legs can "punch through" and destabilize the rig.

While we were performing preloading at one of the

locations we were setting up on, there was a report of a jack-up rig in some other part of the world suffering a "punch-through" with the rig subsequently toppling over into the sea. I made sure from then on that I was always on the deck when "pre-loading" operations were being done, and not in my bed asleep. If the rig was going to topple over into the sea I wanted to be in a position to "jump ship" rather than go down with it!

It was pretty easy to make friends on the rig as everyone was very friendly and got along well together. The food was fantastic so definitely no complaints there. After getting to know one of the roughnecks, Darren, I discovered that he had previously worked for Rockdril with Gary, which made me realize how small a world it is. We had a laugh when we realized the unexpected connection.

After working for 28 days straight it was finally time to fly home – and I've never looked more forward to a break! It was the first time I had ever been away for that long, and with Gary also working away it meant I had a baby-sitter looking after the kids the whole time. It was tough on all of us but I had a couple of months off after that job before going to the next one so we all had plenty of time to recover from it.

Chapter 10

2003 - 2005

TIMOR SEA

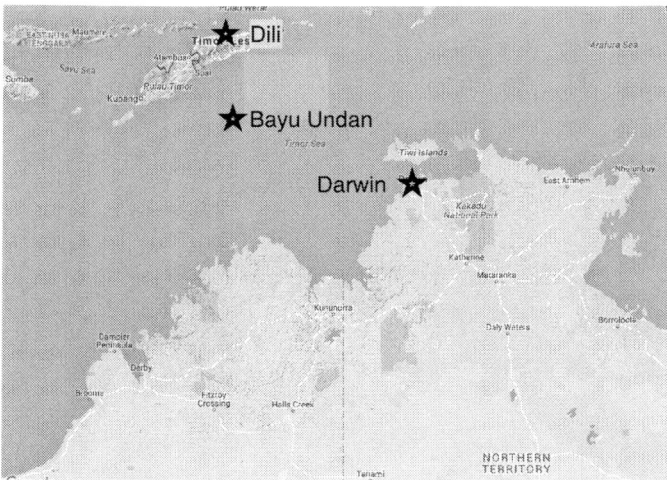

My next hitch offshore was to the Ensco 104, which was another jack-up rig drilling at the Bayu-Undan gas and condensate field in the Joint Petroleum Development Area (JPDA) of the Timor Sea. The JPDA is an area in which Australia and Timor-Leste work together to facilitate the development of shared petroleum resources.

Discovered in 1995, the Bayu-Undan field is a gas-condensate field located 250 km southwest of Suai in Timor-Leste and 500 km northwest of Darwin in Australia. ConocoPhillips operates the field.

At the time of my arrival in the JPDA, the Bayu-Undan

field was in the final stages of setting up a central production and processing complex (CPP), a Floating, Storage and Offloading facility (FSO) 2 km from the CPP and an un-manned wellhead platform (WP1) 7 km east of the CPP. There was also a temporary accommodation platform to house the high number of people needed in the construction phase of the operations. This first phase of the Bayu-Undan operation would also see a total of 13 wells drilled for production, gas injection and water disposal.

Due to the joint agreement with the East Timorese government all crew movements had to be done through Dili, on the northern coast of East Timor, which meant we had to fly in a fixed wing aircraft from Darwin to Dili and then take the chopper from Dili to the rig.

Most of the crew resided in Perth so they had to fly to Darwin the day before their crew change in time to make the 5am check-in at Darwin airport the next morning. As I lived only 40 km away from the Darwin airport in Humpty Doo I gained an extra night's sleep in my own bed.

The flight to Dili was in a commercial Air North scheduled flight so there were also members of the public on the flights, not just rig workers. After an hour on the small plane we disembarked at Dili International Airport and were led off the plane to the heliport facility that was set up next to the main terminal building.

Dili at the time was still in a period of political unease, with the country having had a checkered past since it was originally settled in about 1520 by the Portuguese, who made it the capital of Portuguese Timor in 1769. During World War II it was attacked and occupied by the Japanese in 1942 but in 1945 control of the island was officially returned to Portugal by the Japanese. East Timor was declared independent from Portugal in 1975; however, only nine days later Indonesian forces invaded Dili and annexed East Timor as a province of Indonesia. A guerrilla war ensued from 1975 to 1999 between Indonesian and pro-independence forces, during which tens of thousands of East Timorese were killed. In 1999, East Timor was placed under UN supervision and in 2002 Dili became the capital of the newly independent Democratic Republic of Timor-Leste.

When I arrived in Dili for the first time in September of 2003 there was still a very strong United Nations presence in the city with peacekeeping forces from several UN-aligned nations from around the world having military bases set up within the city. It felt more like we had landed in a military base rather than a civil airport, given the amount of UN helicopters parked on the tarmac. Despite the apparent peacefulness of the tiny third-world community there was definitely an undercurrent of unease that greeted you as you stepped out of the plane on your arrival.

The ConocoPhillips ground logistics was overseen by two supervisors who worked back-to-back on a 2-week rotation from their home bases in Perth. They were supported by another Aussie who lived in Dili permanently with her Australian husband who was an aid worker living in Dili. The rest of the people who worked at the heliport were local East Timorese people who had been trained especially for the role, as were many more who worked out on the rig.

Once our bags arrived at the heliport from the Air North flight they were examined for any contraband items that were forbidden to be taken offshore, such as weapons and explosives. While mobile phones were allowed to be taken out, they had to be handed in to the logistics crew at Dili and they were carried out in a separate bag and held in an office on the rig until your departure at the end of your hitch. There was no wifi on the rig back then, and certainly no cellular network service, so you didn't really have any use for it anyway. In 2003 mobile phones were still only capable of being used to make phone calls, send txt messages or use as an alarm; phones weren't so "smart" back then.

Once our bags were checked and phones handed in (and cigarettes, if you were a smoker) we underwent mandatory alcohol breath testing and random drugs testing via a urine sample. After the processing and screening was completed we viewed the helicopter briefing video and were allocated a life vest and headphones before being marched out in single file to the awaiting Super Puma that would take us out to the rig.

The Ensco 104 was built in 2002 so was quite a new rig when I first arrived on it. It looked luxurious compared to the Ensco 53 that I'd previously been on. I was lucky enough to share a 2-man room with another female Sperry Sun mudlogger who worked on the opposite shift to me so we were always in the room alone, while the other person was on shift. While the room was small and I still had to sleep in a bunk bed, we had our own ensuite bathroom, which more than made up for the cramped conditions.

A tour of the rig during my induction took in all the amenities in the accommodation block and I was excited to see a gymnasium with all new equipment; while it was a very small room and very cramped, it still had good equipment and all I'd need for a decent workout. Although the gym had a treadmill I preferred to run outside on the helideck at the time so my daily cardio session would once again be around in circles up on the helideck before heading to the gym for a weights session.

Once out on the deck I was shown to the muddlogging unit, which was on a level below the drillfloor at the aft end of the rig. The derrick was extended out on a cantilever over the Bayu-Undan central production and processing complex, while drilling a series of production wells through slots that were engineered into the platform below. Because there would eventually be a flare boom operating once production began, the derrick was covered in a heavy canvas sheath to protect the structure from the searing heat the flare would produce. Beyond the processing platform, the huge ship that housed the floating, storage and offloading facility could be seen just 2 km away and to the east you could see the un-manned wellhead platform, WP1.

Mudlogging Unit

Once the induction was done it was straight to work at getting up to speed with the operations. The shift I worked varied from hitch-to-hitch but it was either midday to midnight or midnight to midday. The shift was broken up with a short break for morning tea, lunch and afternoon tea of about 15 minutes for each, although if we were drilling fast then sometimes you wouldn't have time for a break and you'd just have to wait until you finished your shift to be able to sit down in the galley for a meal.

The rig had two change/locker rooms, one on the port side and one on the starboard side, but the men used them both so there was no dedicated "women's" change room. While you were on shift you had to use the toilets in the change rooms because you couldn't go into your bedroom while the other person was sleeping. There were only ever 1 to 3 women on board at any one time so you got used to walking into the bathroom while the men were changing and showering. Needless to say the toilets were usually in a disgusting state, with over 100 men sharing the few toilets that were in the change rooms – and the toilet seat was always up!

****

The Bayu-Undan gas condensate field was discovered

in early 1995 with the drilling of the Bayu-1 well by Phillips Petroleum Company. Four months later BHP Petroleum Pty Ltd drilled the Undan-1 well, 10 km northwest of the Bayu-1 well.

The field is in the northern part of the Bonaparte Basin within the structurally complex Sahul platform, and is the largest petroleum project in operation in the Timor Sea. After the construction phase, which was still in progress when I arrived on the Ensco 104 for the first time, production commenced in 2004 as a gas recycle project - with liquids (condensate, propane and butane) being stripped from the raw production stream, piped to the nearby FSO for storage and then exported. Gas was pumped back down into the reservoir via reinjection wells, which the Ensco 104 drilled. At around the same time, construction commenced on a 500 km subsea natural gas pipeline connecting the Bayu-Undan processing facility to a liquefied natural gas plant situated at Wickham Point in Darwin harbour. I was on the rig when the pipe-laying vessel completed the laying and tying back of this pipeline to the Bayu-Undan processing facility. It was a major milestone in the operation.

Once the Darwin LNG plant would be completed in 2005, gas produced offshore at Bayu-Undan would be transported to the Darwin plant and converted into a liquid and exported.

With the commencement of the production at the facility we saw the flare boom roar to life. A small flame could always be seen at the end of the boom but if there was ever any suspected operational emergency on the production platform then the processing lines would be immediately purged and the gas burnt off via the flare line. With the muddlogging unit being positioned on the aft starboard side of the rig we were right next to the flare boom and the thunderous roar and heat from the flame was extraordinary. Generally an event like this would be accompanied with emergency alarms sounding and we would need to muster in the rig's accommodation block until the emergency was investigated and the facility deemed safe.

****

With the rig only having a capacity of 110 beds there was a shortage of bed space during certain operations when extra crews would be needed. Through such operations, like running and cementing casing, the non-essential personal during that stage of the drilling program were flown off the rig and held on standby in Dili. The mudloggers and wellsite geologists were always the first off and we would get to spend some time checking out the sites in Dili.

On one such occasion I was lucky enough to be in town for the inaugural running of the First Lady's 10km charity fun run in June 2004. Although I'd usually only run about 5 km I thought it would be fun to take part in the celebrations along with fellow mudlogger Dan Walding and wellsite geologists Srdjan Jovanovic and Antonio Ribeiro. We congregated with other competitors on the steps in the square in front of the Palácio do Governo, where the run would start. It was a warm morning and it only promised to get much hotter as we ran the 5 km out and back along the coastal road to the end of the peninsular where the Cristo Rei of Dili sits on top of a globe on top of the headland. The 27-metre tall statue of Jesus is one of the town's landmarks and was a present from the Indonesian Government during the occupation for the 20th anniversary of East Timor's integration into Indonesia.

The run was tough in the tropical heat but the locals came out in force to support the runners, as did the UN troops, so the atmosphere was very festive with the run culminating in a party on the foreshore in Dili. Coming in 7th place out of the women made me one of the top ten women who were presented with a certificate by the run's patron, the First Lady of East Timor, Kirsty Sword Gusmao. It was great getting the opportunity to be involved in such a fantastic community event in the fledgling nation and spending the day celebrating with the locals.

We worked a 3-week rotation for the 20 months I was working at Bayu-Undan so after three weeks on the rig I would then have a three-week break at home. During my breaks at home I continued to take aerobics classes at the local gym and by 2004 the Australian fitness industry governing body increased the accreditation requirements for gym instructors to a Certificate III course and for personal trainers you had to have a Certificate IV in Fitness. I achieved both of these after completing a comprehensive correspondence course over several months which now meant I was accredited, and registered in, group fitness classes, gym floor supervision, nutrition and personal training - an accreditation I'm still registered with today through continual fitness industry education.

****

After nearly two years of working a three-week rotation on

139

the Ensco 104 I had worked myself into a consistent routine of "train-work-eat sleep". Wearing earplugs to bed to block out all the noises in the accommodation block while you were trying to sleep meant I was fearful of sleeping through my alarm but fortunately the "utilities" (room cleaners, laundry washers, dish washes and all round top guys who you never wanted to get on the wrong side of) would give you wake-up calls if needed so it was always nice to get woken up by a cheery utility who would also bring my washing in for me out of the corridor.

On all offshore facilities the utilities do your washing for you every day. At the end of your shift you place your dirty work clothes in a laundry bag and place it on the floor in the corridor outside your bedroom door and it's picked up, washed, dried, folded and placed back in the bag on the floor in front of your room by the time you get up for your next shift. For a mother of three kids, and a husband who counts as a fourth kid when it comes to housework, there is no greater joy than having all the washing, cooking and cleaning done for you.

It wasn't unusual to be the only female on the rig of about 110 personnel, with everyone working and living in extremely close quarters. The best thing about the utility bringing my clothes into my room for me with my wake-up call each morning was that it meant I didn't have to open my door while semi-naked after I got out of bed to retrieve my laundry bag. To this day I still worry about whether there's going to be anyone in the corridor when I open my door so I turn my room light off before opening the door just far enough to reach my arm through and grab the bag and quickly retreat into the dark room. As luck would have it on many occasions, the clothes are placed to the side of the doorway which has me on my hands and knees and trying to reach for my clothes and exposing the least amount of my upper body as I do so. I often wonder if they place it there to avoid a tripping hazard in front of your doorway or just to make you have to leave the safety of your darkened room to grab it. I'm probably setting myself up now and on future jobs I won't be surprised if I find my laundry bag at least a metre down the corridor from my door so I have to make a flying dash into the brightly-lit corridor to retrieve my clothes!

It was inevitable that one day I was going to have a full frontal encounter with one of my fellow workers. Equally unsurprising was the fact that the guys didn't have nearly as big a fear as me of getting caught retrieving their laundry bag from outside their door. To my relief, when it happened it was at least with one of the younger and fitter guys so the unexpected sight of a naked man facing me in the corridor as I turned a corner didn't scar me for life…in fact I think it actually made my day. We both momentarily balked at the sight of each other then broke out into a huge smile and continued on our way as if nothing had happened. Not being one to shy away from making a big deal of an awkward situation, before the morning pre-work meeting I printed out a mock certificate that I instructed the convener of the meeting to present to this guy as an award for picking the worst possible timing for collecting his washing from the corridor while totally naked. It brought a smile to everyone's faces at the end of the usually mundane meeting.

The "pre-tour" meeting was held in the dining area of

the galley prior to the commencement of every 12-hour shift, to get everyone up-to-speed on what had happened in the previous 12 hours while they were not working. Meetings are taken very seriously offshore and not only are the daily pre-tour meetings and the weekly safety meetings mandatory, but you also have to sign an attendance sheet at each meeting to prove you have attended. One day during the conclusion of the pre-tour meeting I was sitting to the right of a guy who had a bit of a personality disposition and one of his fellow crew members who was sitting to his left wrote his name down for him and also followed it with a smart-arse comment about him. I'm not sure what it was but it immediately got him fired up and he became enraged and grabbed the guy sitting beside him by the front of his shirt and pushed him up against the wall. I quickly jumped out of the way and watched on in amusement at the testosterone-fuelled jostling in the crowded galley. It got broken up nearly as quickly as it started but it provided a bit of entertainment at the start of an otherwise boring, routine day.

Not only were meetings mandatory, but also the writing of at least one safety observation card – "STOP" card as they were referred to – was mandatory and at one stage they become such a safety focus that you would even be hunted down in your room and woken up if you hadn't submitted one before midnight each day.

At one stage, the office in Perth accidentally sent out two large rolls of photographic paper for the plotter that was used to print the well-path plans and one enterprising directional driller (you know who you are Tommy) went into business printing full-size photos of naked models found on the internet and selling them to the drill crew in exchange for ready-written STOP cards. The warm electrical wiring space in the wall of his office was used as a drying cupboard and it had naked women hanging from the roof until they were dry enough to be pinned on the back of someone's bathroom door. It was all done very covertly of course!

The drilling program on the Ensco 104 wound up in 2005 and I did my last hitch on the rig in April 2005. Unfortunately Sperry Sun had no other muddlogging contracts working out of Australia so after a few weeks at home I decided to follow the other mudloggers over to the UK and work in the North Sea on another ConocoPhillips job that was utilizing mudloggers out of Sperry Sun's Aberdeen base.

By this stage, Gary had been working for Boart-Longyear for a few years and was based in their Chiang Mai office in Thailand. He came home on regular breaks every couple of months but I desperately wanted to take Alex and Becky over there and have all of us living together in Thailand as expats, like many of Gary's drilling mates had done with their families. Christopher had already left home by this stage and was working as an offsider on mineral rigs in the Central Queensland coalfields, working FIFO out of Brisbane. Gary was very much against a family move to Chiang Mai as he wanted his home base to remain in Australia but after much nagging from me it was decided that we'd all move over there during the mid year school holidays so the kids could start school at the Prem Tinsulanonda International School at the start of their school year in August.

With the big move coming up I was only expecting to do one hitch away in the North Sea because I would then be busy settling the kids and myself into our new life in Thailand, and my career going on hold again for a while.

Chapter 11

2005

NORTH SEA, UK

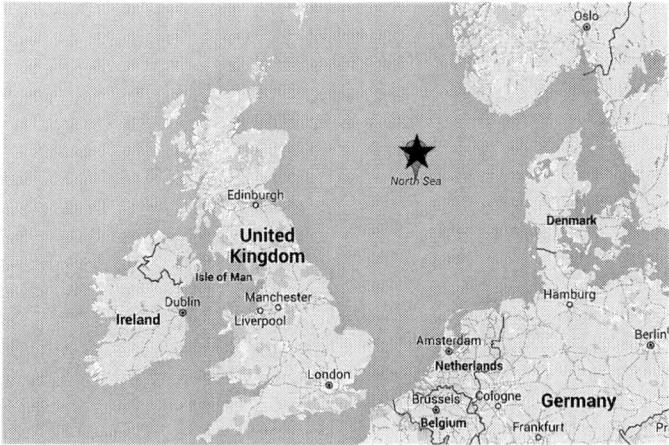

Arriving in Aberdeen after the long trip from Darwin, I checked into the hotel in Dyce that had been booked for me. It was the middle of spring, but the weather was certainly colder than what I was used to in Darwin and the Timor Sea. It was a nice sunny day on my arrival but there certainly wasn't much heat in the sun.

After dropping my gear off in my room I caught a taxi to the Sperry Sun (Halliburton) office in Dyce to meet the crew who worked in the office I'd be working from. The office and equipment yard were conveniently located close to the airport where the heliports that service the North

Sea offshore operations are based.

The next three days were spent doing another BOSIET course, but this time a cold-water one which would include training in the use of emergency breathing system equipment and wearing an immersion suit, things that weren't done in the tropical version of the sea survival course that I'd done in Perth two years earlier. The re-breather is a bladder with a mouthpiece that you wear over the top of your life jacket, which is also worn over the watertight survival suit. It's designed to be breathed into with one deep breath of air from your lungs and then you can use that air to give you a few minutes of oxygen to survive long enough under water to escape an overturned helicopter.

The sea survival part of the course was done with our immersion suits on and unfortunately the suits used at the training facility were old discarded industry ones and the sizes were very limited. With most men who work offshore in the North Sea being a lot bigger than me, there were no small sizes in the suits and I ended up having to wear a large one. The basic principle of a survival suit is that they are to be airtight so no water can get into them if you are stranded in the water. You step into the suit without your shoes on and then pull it up over your shoulders and squeeze your head through an opening that has a rubber seal like a wetsuit, and the wrists also have the same rubber seal to ensure the suit is watertight. You then put your shoes back on over the outside of the suits feet. Having to wear a large suit meant that the wrist and neck seals were too loose to prevent water getting into the suit so as soon as I jumped into the pool the suit started to fill up with water. Fortunately we had flotation devices on over the top of the immersion suit which prevented me from sinking to the bottom of the pool but it made it very hard to perform the sea survival exercises when I weighed twice as much as I normally do. The last part of the sea survival drills was simulating getting winched out of the water with a strop and as I was pulled further out of the water the suit ballooned out with its extra weight and when I was laid out on the poolside I felt, and looked, like a beached whale. With no opening at the feet I had to unzip the top part of the suit, roll over onto my side, and get someone to raise my legs off the ground so the water would drain down through the opening near my chest. Needless to say I was very glad when I finally got the course over and done with.

The next morning I checked in at the heliport for the flight out to the Maersk Inspirer jack-up rig that was preparing to start drilling over the Judy Platform in the J-Block field in the central North Sea.

The distances, number of workplaces and fierce weather in the 750,000 square kilometres (290,000 square miles) of the North Sea area have resulted in the operation of the world's largest fleet of heavy instrument flight rules (IFR) helicopters, some specifically developed for the North Sea. They carry about two million passengers per year from 16 onshore bases, of which Aberdeen Airport is the world's busiest with 500,000 passengers per year.

The chopper flight out to the rig took over an hour and a half and the rubber seals on the wrists of my immersion suit were so tight I had to keep pulling on them to relieve the pain they were causing, and prevent the circulation from being cut-off to my hands. As well as the immersion suit, the life jacket and the re-breather, we were required to wear three layers of clothes under our suits, so to say the trip was uncomfortable would be a gross understatement.

The North Sea is a marginal sea of the Atlantic Ocean located between Great Britain, Scandinavia, Germany, the Netherlands, Belgium, and France. It connects to the ocean through the English Channel in the south and the Norwegian Sea in the north.

Until the 1960s all UK oil supplies were imported but after the UK Continental Shelf Act came into force in May 1964, seismic exploration began and the first offshore well followed later that year. It and a second well on the Mid North Sea High were dry, but BP's Sea Gem rig struck gas in the West Sole Field in September 1965. Unfortunately the celebrations were short-lived because the Sea Gem sank with the loss of 13 lives after part of the rig collapsed as it was moved away from the discovery well. The Viking Gas Field was discovered in December 1965 with the Conoco/National Coal Board well 49/17-1, finding the gas-bearing Permian Rotliegend Sandstone at a depth of 2,756 metres subsea. Larger gas finds followed in 1966 but by 1968 companies had lost interest in further exploration of the British sector, a result of a ban on gas exports and low prices offered by the only buyer, British Gas.

The situation was transformed in December 1969, when Phillips Petroleum discovered oil in Chalk of Danian age at Ekofisk, in Norwegian waters in the central North Sea. The same month, Amoco discovered the Montrose Field about 217 km (135 miles) east of Aberdeen. BP had been awarded several licenses in the area in the second licensing round late in 1965, but had been reluctant to work on them. The discovery of Ekofisk prompted them to drill what turned out to be a dry hole in May 1970, followed by the discovery of the giant Forties Oil Field in October 1970. The following year, Shell Expro discovered the giant Brent oilfield in the northern North Sea east of Shetland in Scotland and the Petronord Group discovered the Frigg gas field. The Piper oilfield was discovered in 1973 and the Statfjord Field and the Ninian Field in 1974.

The price of Brent Crude, one of the first types of oil extracted from the North Sea, is used today as a standard price for comparison for crude oil from the rest of the world. The North Sea contains Western Europe's largest oil and natural gas reserves and is one of the world's key non-OPEC producing regions.

Although the production costs are relatively high, the quality of the oil, the political stability of the region, and the nearness of important markets in Western Europe have made the North Sea an important oil-producing region.

World oil prices for 1973–4 were vastly increased by OPEC, making high North Sea production costs viable. Exploration peaked with 80 wells drilled. Supporting manufacturing industries produced and maintained pipelines, rigs, platforms, supply vessels, pumps and cranes, and made the North Sea oil industry 'one of the major industrial achievements of the 20th century'. *(By January 2015, the North Sea would be the world's most active offshore drilling region with 173 active rigs drilling).*

The largest single humanitarian catastrophe in the

North Sea oil industry was the destruction of the offshore oil platform Piper Alpha in 1988 in which 167 people lost their lives. The recommendations from the investigation into the causes of this incident led to the adoption of the Offshore Installations (Safety Case) Regulations 1992 which saw improvements made in the implementation of the "Permit to Work" system. Every induction course you do will invariably show a movie of the Piper Alpha catastrophe as a leading example of what NOT to do while working on equipment in a high-risk environment. While working over the Bayu-Undan gas processing facility it was always in the back of my mind that when something goes wrong on these platforms, it could go *catastrophically* wrong.

The J-Block gas condensate/oil fields are located in the central North Sea. Commercial oil production and natural gas sales from the J-Area's Judy/Joanne fields began in 1997. Gas processed on the Judy Platform is transported through the Central Area Transmission System Pipeline, and liquids are transported to Teesside through the Norpipe System. Judy is the name assigned to the main platform and Joanne the name for the subsea manifold. The Phillips tradition is to name the fields alphabetically, using the name of a female relative of the projects senior geologist.

****

Once we landed on the Maersk Inspirer I completed the rig induction and was shown to my cabin. The immersion suit was kept in the locker in my room and would stay there until it was time to fly off the rig. It was such a relief to get it off after landing and re-establish full blood circulation to my hands.

The Inspirer was (and still is) the world's largest and most advanced ultra-harsh environment jack-up rig. When I landed on deck it still hadn't even had any mud go over the shakers – they were brand spanking new. The accommodation block was as good as it gets offshore with our 2-man cabins having king-size single beds on either side of the spacious room with luxuriously warm *real* feather duvets on the beds. Every room had its own climate control thermostat and the ensuite bathroom had a heated tiled floor, which felt highly decadent for an offshore oilrig.

The never-ending list of amenities continued to amaze me as I explored the accommodation block, with an expansive central staircase being overshadowed by a fully operational lift/elevator. The utilities certainly would have been happy with that. There were also not only men's toilets, but also women's toilets on every level of the accommodation block – what a luxury! There was a dedicated women's change room and the lockers were heated so your clothes and boots would be nice and warm when you put them on. Given that I was about to start working in one of the most unforgiving climates of anywhere around the world I knew I would be needing every bit of heating I could get.

With all the super-sized amenities I was glad to find out the gym was just as generously appointed, albeit lacking a bit of equipment. It was the first job the new rig had been on so they hadn't stocked the gym with much equipment yet but it had a few machines and a treadmill so I was happy. With the weather usually being inhospitable outside most days, any recreational use of the helideck was banned – you wouldn't have lasted long up there in the high winds anyway. It would be only treadmill runs for me for the duration of my stay.

Being a ConocoPhillips job, I was excited to learn the company man who was onboard was the same Houston-based company man who was on the Ensco 104 in the Timor Sea, Stan Rodgers. He was very surprised to see me walk past his office door while on the induction tour of the rig. There was also the Scottish mud engineer from the Timor Sea job on the rig so it was a bit like a re-union for us all.

My first hitch had me working back-to-back with another female Sperry mudlogger Kirsten, an ex-South African-

and-now-Scottish mother of two kids. It was just a shame we only ever saw each other for about 15 minutes at the start and end of each shift. There was also a female wellsite geologist on board, Caroline, and an MWD engineer Kimberley, so there were 4 female geologists on board although Caroline was the only one who actually had a geologist title. The only other female on board the rig was a rigger who worked out on the deck – kudos to her, it was miserable out in that weather!

I shared my room with Kirsten, and later Kat, who was Kirsten's relief and also a female geologist working for Sperry as a mudlogger. It was, and still is, quite common that the only females working on the rigs are either mudloggers or MWD (Measurement While Drilling) engineers. The newer rigs that have female bathroom facilities tend to have some female utilities (cleaners) also, but the older rigs have all male crews both out on the deck and inside the accommodation.

With the summer months approaching the days became very long with the sun not setting until about 11pm at night and rising again at 3am in the height of summer. My first hitch had me working from midnight to midday and it was really strange to walk out of the mudlogging unit at 3am to go for a break and it was already daylight outside.

The mudlogging unit had a phone we could ring out on so I would call the kids most days and talk to them briefly after they got home from school. I was extremely lucky I had such a great babysitter, Margaret, looking after the kids for me on that long hitch away.

The industry standard rotation in the North Sea was 2-weeks on and 2-weeks off so after being on the rig for two weeks I had to leave for a break. I was able to arrange for just one week off so I didn't get stuck away from home for too long on no pay, as it was too expensive to fly me home and back again just for two weeks.

Not wanting to spend my week off in Aberdeen I decided to take advantage of the cheap international flights in that part of the world and booked a 5-day trip the Canary Island of Tenerife. I left the rig with one of the Sperry data engineers, Stewart, who offered for me to stay overnight at his place in Glasgow, as that's where I was flying out of the next morning. It was a lovely train ride down to Glasgow from Aberdeen and I got to see a bit more of the beautiful Scottish countryside while having a break off the rig. But ultimately I wanted to be somewhere warm!

After a week I returned to the Inspirer for another two-week hitch before returning back home to Darwin.

Move to Thailand

With the day fast approaching when we would be making the big move to Thailand, we held a garage sale and sold off everything in our house except a few personal belongings that we would take with us and some other belongings that Gary kept in a storage container on our 20-acre property. The house would get rented out once we left.

Everyone except me was angry about having to make the move; I seemed to be the only one who could see the great opportunity at getting the chance to live in another country. Of course Gary had been doing it for years so was reluctant to change his status quo. Alex and Becky, who were now 16 and 14-years old, definitely weren't looking forward to leaving their friends and having to start at another school. I had my work cut out for me convincing them all of the benefits of the move but I was determined

155

to give it a go. I was so envious of Gary's mate's wives who were living overseas with their husbands as expats in Thailand, Indonesia and Malaysia and bringing their kids up in the International School system. I wanted my kids to have the same opportunity.

I had been over there on a previous trip and booked the kids into the school, and Gary had organized for a rental house in the same residential area that he currently lived in while over there. With us arriving on a Friday and the house not being ready to move into until the following Monday, we planned to stay at the house Gary had been living in which also doubled as the Boart-Longyear office. With the office downstairs, there was a 2-bedroom residence upstairs so we could all squeeze in there for the few days.

With Gary flying over in his company-paid business class seat and me and the kids down the back in economy we got off to a lackluster start. The moods were downright somber and I was starting to feel the first signs of defeat.

When we arrived in Chiang Mai Becky and Alex grew even more despondent but I managed to cheer them up a little after taking them to see the house where we would be living. It was huge and looked like what I imagined an Australian Embassy would look like.

The next day, Saturday, we were all hanging around the office, the kids killing time playing on their laptops through the office wifi, when Alex called out that there was water coming up the driveway. We didn't pay much notice to it at the time but within a few hours the water had risen so much it was now getting close to coming in the house. We were soon to find out that Chiang Mai was about to experience a once-in-30-year flood and the water didn't stop rising until it had submerged the entire downstairs level of the house. We all worked frantically to keep lifting the office furniture and filing cabinets higher out of the encroaching water and retreated to the upstairs rooms to avoid staying in the filthy brown river water that had now flooded the lower floor.

Once the floodwaters reached the house's electrical wiring we not only had no power, but also no water because the water required an electric pump to operate. The day's dramas eventually came to a head with tempers flaring and I realized there was no way my much-wanted move was going to work out. While I knew I had to bite the bullet and give up on my dream of living in Thailand, I also knew I couldn't stand the thought of living in Humpty Doo for the rest of my life and that Gary and I had different ideas of where we were heading. We decided I'd take the kids back to Australia and we'd go our separate ways.

As the afternoon turned into night we all went to bed very early because there was nothing else to do and we were all shell-shocked by the events of the day. We hoped the floodwaters would have gone down overnight but to our horror the next morning, it was still just as deep. We put marks on the windows where the water line was so we could check to see when it started to go down but it wasn't going anywhere very fast.

By the afternoon Gary had to risk walking through the waist-deep water and try and find somewhere to buy food, as we had nothing in the house. We had already seen a snake swim past the lounge room window so knew we needed to stay out of the water if possible. After a couple of hours he returned but all he could find was a fuel station so all he could get were potato crisps, chocolates and soft drinks. At one stage we had someone in a dingy drop off a supply of drinking water and Becky waded outside and retrieved it from the back of Gary's work car, where it had been dropped off.

As night approached we had accepted we would have to spend another night stranded in the upstairs rooms of the house when we suddenly heard someone calling from outside. We looked out a window and there was a dingy with army personal in it shining lights up at us and calling for us to come down and be taken to higher ground. We quickly packed a backpack each and waded out to the boat and climbed onboard. The army had been notified by an employee of Gary's who knew of our predicament and organized for us to get transported to the nearest high ground on the motorway where he could then pick us up and drive us to a hotel in the city.

It was 10pm by the time we got to the hotel and only just made it in time to get a meal in the restaurant. We were starving and in desperate need of proper food and didn't even have time to shower and put clean clothes on. We hadn't showered in two days and looked like crap but we all saw the funny side of eating and staying at a 5-star hotel and looking like homeless people – which we actually were!

After a few days we all flew back to Darwin and set up what little furniture we had put into storage back in the house and the kids and I lived there until I bought a smaller place. Being a single mother with two teenage kids to support now on my own I had to get back to work and was fortunately able to return to my job at the North Sea.

Another friend, and the mother of one of Becky's best friends, offered to take over babysitting duties and stayed in my house with the kids – and her kids – while I did two more 4-week hitches out of the UK, working for 4 weeks then flying back to Australia and having a 4-week break at home and then doing it all again a second time.

My last hitch on the Maersk Inspirer was during November-December so it was now close to winter and very cold when I landed in Aberdeen. After staying overnight in the company house I caught the chopper out to the rig the next morning.

The days were now very short with only about 6 hours of daylight each day. I was working midnight to midday so only saw about 3 hours of daylight while I was on shift. The weather was horrendous with gale force winds most days and freezing cold conditions. I made use of the heated bathroom floor by laying my clothes on it while I was sleeping so they were nice and warm when I put them on after my shower. The heated boot lockers in the change-room were definitely a great idea and it was always a treat slipping my feet into the warmth of my boots before I headed out onto the windswept deck to start my shift each night.

The external entrance to the change-room was on the lower outer deck and there was only a small area that was protected from the wind once you stepped outside the door before you were battered by the weather. Before even leaving the safety of the room you could not only hear the faint howling of the wind outside, but you could feel the rig being buffeted around against the force of it. When you only weigh 50 kg (110 lbs.) you have to be prepared to lean into the wind to be able to brace against it or you risk getting blown off balance – and that would be really embarrassing – so it was a delicate balancing act having to judge before you got out on the open deck, how much to lean into the wind without actually going too far and falling flat on your face. The struggle was real! By the time I got to the mudlogging unit at the aft end of the rig I would be exhausted – and I still had a 12-hour shift to go.

I was on shift with Stewart again, who was the Sperry Data Engineer. Everyone else who worked in the mudlogging unit was Scottish – except me. Although I was familiar with the Scottish accent, it wasn't until I actually worked in Scotland that I realized that many of the Scots have such a strong accent it sounds like they're talking a foreign language. With such a multi-national workforce on the rig it wasn't unusual to have a southern Texan and a regional Scotsman talking in the pre-tour meetings and not be able to understand a word either of them was saying. We all supposedly spoke English but damn, some of those accents were bloody strong.

While I was working on the Inspirer there was work being done on the Judy Platform by contracting crews who were flown on to perform the scheduled maintenance. With a skills shortage in the industry it looked like they were pulling people out of retirement to get the job done because many of the workers were middle-aged and very overweight and looked like they were about to have a stroke. I asked Stewart if there were ever any deaths in the industry from people being unfit for the job but it was really just a pointed comment rather than a question.

While many of the jobs performed on offshore facilities don't require brute strength to perform, just getting around the decks can be taxing on the cardiovascular system. Not only is it a big area but there are also many levels and many steep, metal staircases to climb to get around. In fact, many of them are so steep it would probably be more appropriate to call them ladders. It can be very taxing on the cardiovascular system if you continually have to negotiate these stairs to get around within work sites. It seemed like a good reason for me to stay fit. And I was soon to realize how important this would be.

During one of my pre-work gym sessions I was laying on the floor doing some post-workout stretching when the rig medic walked into the room and retrieved a big vinyl pouch from a stores cupboard at the end of the room. As he walked past me with it in his hand I made a general comment asking how he was and he replied, in a somber tone, "I've got a body". After returning a puzzled look to him he qualified his previous statement and said: "I've got a dead body" and as he raised the package he was holding I realized that it must have been a "body bag" - and it was soon going to have a corpse in it. The first thing I thought of were the few men who I had been feeling uncomfortable about whether they were fit for the job and it seems my fears were justified.

When we were assembled for the 11:30pm pre-tour meeting the announcement was made that one of the contractors had felt unwell during his lunch break and laid down in his room but never returned. His dead body was later found on his bed. The police had been flown out to the rig during the afternoon to do an investigation before the body was flown off the rig but otherwise it was work as usual. The police, and the dead body, would stay on the rig overnight and then be flown off the next day.

It all seemed a bit surreal going out to start work after being told news like that. Because the deceased man was not part of the regular rig crew, he wasn't known to anybody so there was really a bit of disconnect with the whole situation. There was no work-place accident involved and it was nobody's fault so it was just an unfortunate occurrence.

So once I got out to the mudlogging unit at midnight it was work as usual, at least I thought it was until a couple of hours later when all the power on the rig cut and left us in total darkness except for the few emergency lights scattered around the place. Normally when there's a power failure the emergency back-up power will automatically kick in, but for some strange reason it didn't happen.

For safety reasons mudlogging units are pressurized so the air pressure inside the unit is higher than that outside the unit. Because of the close proximity to the drillfloor and the shakers (where the returns from the drillhole come to surface), the unit is in the most hazardous zone on the rig should there be any uncontrolled gas encountered while drilling. Positive pressurization helps prevent contamination of the air within the unit, thereby maintaining a safe working environment not only for the personnel but also for the sensitive monitoring equipment contained within the unit. There is generally an air lock at the entry to the unit so the inner door doesn't have to be opened until the outer door is closed, preventing any appreciable decrease in the pressurization upon entry to the unit. For safety requirements, all the power to the unit automatically shuts down if the pressure of the unit drops below a certain allowance for longer than a minute. Once the equipment is "powered down" there is quite a lengthy procedure to get it all up and running again so it is avoided at all costs. This is why visitors to the mudlogging unit who aren't aware of this situation and absent-mindedly don't close the doors properly behind them when entering, will get yelled at by the crew inside who frantically shove you aside as they rush to shut the outside door before the whole unit powers down.

So getting back to the power outage on the rig…at first we just thought it was a temporary glitch in the rig power and fully expected the power to come back on within a minute, even if it was the auxiliary power supply, but as the time wore on there was no resumption and eventually the mudlogging unit completely shut down. I've seen the rig power go down before as it's not that uncommon, but I'd never seen the rig power go down and the auxiliary power *not* come on pretty well straight away. The offshore rigs are so highly sophisticated these days that they're run almost completely on electrical systems, so any power failure means expensive delays and potentially devastatingly dangerous situations should they be drilling through a reservoir at the time of failure. For this reason they always have a back-up emergency power supply that kicks in within seconds of the main power supply being interrupted. But this didn't happen this time.

We all stood outside the mudlogging unit and looked back towards the accommodation block and there was only silenced darkness – never have I been on a rig and been in total silence – it was the eeriest thing I'd ever witnessed. The only lights that could be seen were the small last-resort emergency lights that lead you to the lifeboats. After waiting and watching for a few minutes we decided to make our way to the accommodation block and see if we could find out what was going on. The only place that was fairly well lit was the galley so we sat in there while everyone scratched their heads in wonder and waited for the power to be restored. It ended up taking over an hour before the heartbeat of the rig came back to life and everything was back up and running. Dead body on board…unexplained total power failure…. hmmm, it was all pretty weird!

Six months after my first trip to the North Sea I was

heading home for the last time. The rotation out of the UK was a bit too hard to manage for me, and the poor babysitters who helped me out. I was away for nearly 5 weeks each trip with the travel taken into account so I really needed to find something a bit closer to home. It was only a few days before Christmas and there was snow falling at the Aberdeen airport while I was sitting on the plane waiting to take off for my flight home. It looked pretty out the window but I was glad to be getting out of the cold and heading back to tropical Darwin.

Once I got home I started to contact other mudlogging service companies and managed to get a job with Geoservices who still had plenty of work on the offshore rigs around Australia. Eventually I headed off to work down in Bass Strait where the rotation was 2 weeks on, 2 weeks off, a much more family-friendly roster.

Bass Strait is approximately 350 km wide and 500 km long, with an average depth of 60 metres and a maximum depth of 83 metres.

Like the rest of the waters surrounding Tasmania, and particularly because of its limited depth, it's notoriously rough, with many ships lost there during the 19th century. A lighthouse was erected on Deal Island in 1848 to assist ships in the eastern part of the Straits, but there were no guides to the western entrance until the Cape Otway Lighthouse was first lit in 1848, followed by another at Cape Wickham at the northern end of King Island in 1861.

Victoria's oil and gas exploration and production is concentrated in the offshore Commonwealth waters of the Otway and Gippsland basins, and to a lesser extent in the Bass Basin. While the Otway and Gippsland basins have an onshore and an offshore component, with exploration for oil and gas being done for around 100 years in the onshore parts of both basins, the majority of oil and gas discoveries and production to date have been from the offshore regions of the basins. Relatively small amounts of gas have been produced from conventional traps in the onshore Otway Basin.

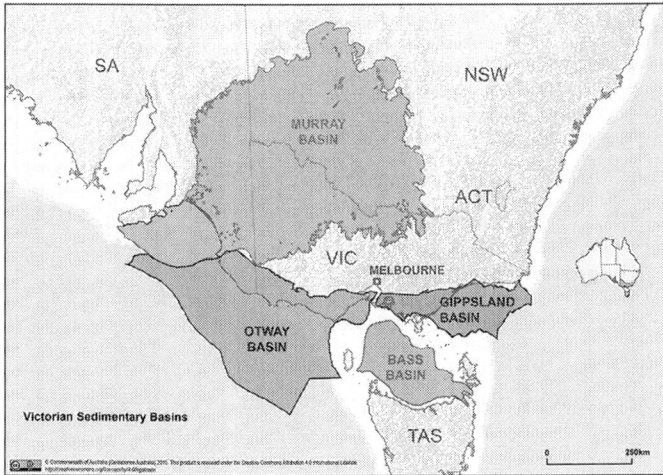

Victorian Sedimentary Basins

The offshore Gippsland Basin has been the source of significant oil and gas production since the late 1960s. Conventional petroleum resources have been discovered in structural and combined structural and stratigraphic traps, mostly within Late Cretaceous to Eocene clastic sequences.

The Otway Basin covers approximately 150,000km, extending along the southern margin of Victoria and South Australia to the northwest of Tasmania with eighty per cent of the basin being offshore.

The first wells in the Victorian part of the Otway Basin were drilled in the 1920s to 1940s in the Anglesea and Torquay areas. The Otway Basin has been the source of a number of important gas discoveries, particularly in the offshore Shipwreck Trough and the onshore Port Campbell Embayment.

In 1965, after overcoming the many technical challenges of

drilling offshore and with the extremely hostile weather conditions, BHP and Esso drilled Australia's first offshore well in Bass Strait. The well successfully encountered hydrocarbons and discovered the Barracouta gas field. Additional gas bearing reservoirs were located in 1966 and oil was discovered in 1967. Through these discoveries, BHP confirmed that Bass Strait was a world-class hydrocarbon province.

The discovery of oil and gas in Bass Strait was a watershed moment in the history of Australia and BHP, with BHP being transformed from a steel maker and a mining company to a serious player in the offshore oil industry. It also provided Australia with a degree of energy independence and self-sufficiency previously unimaginable.

There are now 23 offshore platforms and installations in Bass Strait which feed a network of 600 km of underwater pipelines and keep the oil and gas flowing, 24 hours a day.

****

My first 2-week hitch with Geoservices was to be spent on the semi-submersible rig, the Ocean Patriot, in Bass Strait. I'd only ever worked on jack-up rigs before so I was a bit concerned about whether the slight movement on the floating rig would cause me any problems with seasickness.

A semi-submersible rig is supported by pontoon-type columns that are submerged into the water. The design concept of partially submerging the rig lessens both rolling and pitching on "semisubs". They are towed into position and anchored, and kept in position by their own azimuth thrusters with dynamic positioning.

My trip to the rig started from Essendon airport in Melbourne, where we would board the helicopter to take us out to the rig that was drilling in the offshore Gippsland Basin in Bass Strait. The heliport was a far cry from the huge facility I had previously been flying out of in Aberdeen. The small office had a room where we viewed the mandatory chopper safety briefing and then a rack of immersion suits was wheeled into the main office and everyone had to grab a suit and put it on. There were only about twenty suits to choose from and none of them were small sizes. I had to take a medium sized suit, which of course was a medium "men's" size, not women's, so it was very big on me and the wrist and neck rubber seals definitely didn't "seal". The heavy canvas suit hung from me like an over-sized sack and I knew exactly what would happen if I ended up in the water while wearing it. With no option other than wearing it or being sent home with no job, I just prayed the chopper stayed in the air and didn't ditch into the sea before it got to the rig. It seems that even sophisticated safety systems can overlook the obvious.

The chopper ride took us right over the eastern suburbs of Melbourne and all the way over land until we got to Longford airport in Gippsland where it landed to re-fuel, before flying the final 50 km over Bass Strait to the rig. Once we landed we had to take our suits off and leave them in a room out on the deck.

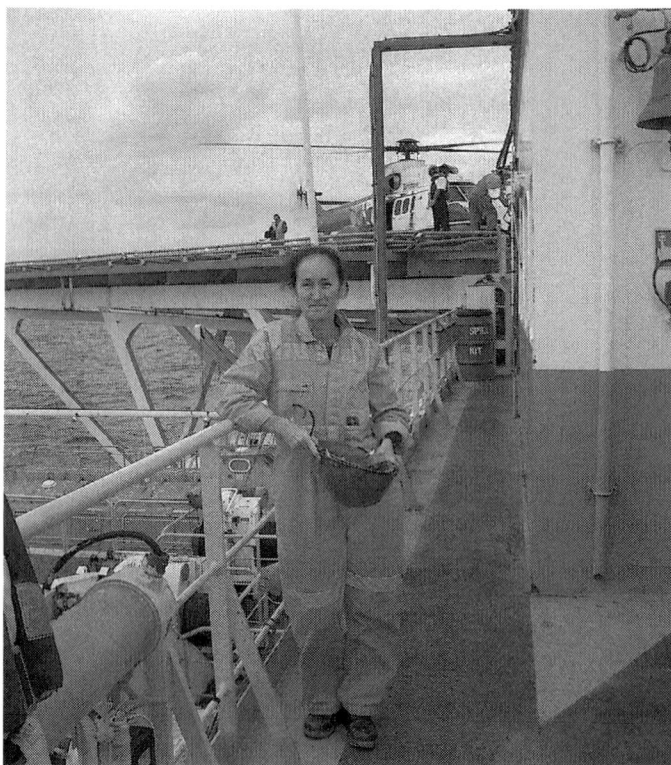

After a routine rig induction I headed out to the mudlogging unit and met the Geoservices crew that I'd be working with. To my surprise there was also a Sperry MWD and directional drilling crew on board and two of them were people I'd worked with as mudloggers on the Ensco 104 in the Timor Sea six months earlier. Belinda and Sam were just as surprised to see me there working for Geoservices as I was of seeing them in their new roles. I managed to get a photo of them as they were leaving for the chopper at the end of their hitch, which is always the best time to get a smile for the camera!

The well we were on was getting drilled for Anzon Australia in the Manta field, which was one of a group of fields operated by Anzon known as the Basker, Manta and Gummy fields (the BMG Fields). My second hitch to the rig would be in the Basker field and these were both development wells, which would be producing oil and gas later in 2006.

Oil resources in the BMG fields comprised stacked pay in numerous thin sands within the Late Cretaceous/Tertiary Latrobe Group with multiple contacts and trapped by internal seals. The sands were typically good reservoir quality. Gas resources in the BMG fields comprised gas in the Latrobe sands and in the deeper Late Cretaceous Golden Beach zones.

The mudlogging unit was smaller than what I had previously worked in while working for Sperry because it only housed the sample catchers, mudloggers, data engineers and wellsite geologist, while the MWD and directional drillers who were contracted through Sperry, not Geoservices, had their own unit.

The smaller unit meant an even more confined place to work, but being stuck inside a small shipping container full of monitoring equipment for twelve hours a day was what this job was all about so you just had to make the most of it. With such a claustrophobic work environment it's essential that everyone works together as a team as personality clashes can make or break you in this job. It's not unusual to have several nations represented in one mudlogging unit, which just helps, make it an even more interesting place to work. I'm sure there's no other workplace in the world where people from so many different countries and cultures, fly from all around the world to do a two-to-four week hitch then fly all the way home again. Everyone works together as one team while on board the rig, regardless of your nationality, race, culture, religion, marital status and gender.

Life on the rig was definitely made easier however, by the incredibly good food that the cooks delivered. All the main meals were worthy of a Michelin star rating and the cooks even took enormous pride in the presentation of the food. Like all rigs, the buffet-style meals were also complimented with a fridge full of deserts that you could help yourself to any time of the day or night. A dangerous indulgence that most succumb to offshore. Which gets me onto the gym. While it was extremely small, it was well equipped and meant I could maintain my usual training regime. To give you an idea of how cramped it was, the length of the treadmill was the same distance as the width of the room. The front of the treadmill was touching one wall and the back of the treadmill was up against the other wall, with a TV mounted on the wall in front of it which was so close to your face it was difficult to focus on. With a brand newish set of free weights, a Smith Machine, a treadmill, rower and bike there was everything you needed for a decent workout – you just had to hope no-one else wanted to train at the same time because the room was overcrowded with any more than one person in it. Fortunately for me most people preferred to train in the gym *after* their shift, not *before* it, so I generally had it to myself. Recreational activities were not allowed on the helideck due to the often-extreme weather conditions so the treadmill was now my only choice for running.

The pre-tour meeting was held in the TV room before the start of every shift and in the case of my shift, the timing of it just happened to coincide with a TV show about Lithuanian women wrestling in a pool of honey in their bikinis. As you can probably guess, the bikinis quite often "fell" off, much to the delight of the mustered crew who were waiting for the start of the meeting. Being the only female in the room I was definitely out-numbered when it came to choosing the TV programs.

During the second week of my hitch the weather started deteriorating, with the sea getting quite rough and a huge swell developing. The supply boat that sits alongside the rig would disappear one moment then pop back up in view from the deck of the rig the next, as it rode the crests and troughs of the swell. Being a "floater", the rig had a bit of movement on it but it was surprisingly stable given the size of the swell. I didn't feel seasick at all so I was very grateful I'd passed that test.

While asleep in bed during the bad weather, I was awoken to the sound of the fire alarm. We have a fire drill every Sunday to practice the emergency mustering and rig abandonment procedures but it wasn't Sunday so I was hoping it was just a false alarm and waited for the announcement saying we could ignore the alarm so I could go back to sleep. With our room being on the lowest deck I could hear the sound of the waves crashing against the underside of the rig. I knew that if there was ever going to be an emergency that would require us to abandon the rig then it was most probably going to be in really bad weather. The thought of getting lowered down in the lifeboats into that surging sea in the black of night was horrifying so I was praying it was a false alarm and it would be sorted out really soon and a PA announcement made. But no, there was no announcement, so I knew I had to start making my way to the muster station. I quickly threw some clothes on and headed out into the corridor and joined the other sleepy people who were looking a bit shell-shocked. No one seemed to know what was happening so we had to take it seriously and assume it was not a false alarm and that there was actually an emergency situation on the rig. Just as I got to the end of the corridor there was finally a PA announcement saying that it was a false alarm and we could ignore it. Phew, I hoped that's as close as I ever have to get to abandoning a rig!

With the arrival of fly-out day, also came the unwelcomed arrival of gale force winds in Bass Strait. The outgoing crew (including me) were briefed for departure but the news came through that the chopper wasn't leaving the shore base because the winds were too strong for landing on the helideck of the rig. As the morning wore on the winds only seemed to be getting stronger and the seas rougher but there was still hope of us getting off the rig at some stage. Despite the foul weather, fly-out day is fly-out day and all you want to do is get on the chopper and go home. Everyone was still hopeful of the chopper coming out and eventually it did, but then as I started to walk up the staircase to the helideck to board the aircraft I became aware of how strong the wind actually was up there and I started to doubt if I had enough bodyweight to keep me from flying off the deck, or at least off my feet. I had visions of men either side of me grabbing my hands as my legs flew out from under me and my body flying parallel to the deck, like a human windsock! Now I was starting to get scared. Did I really want to be flying in a helicopter, over water, in such horrible conditions? The conditions today were even worse than what I'd experienced in the North Sea. Now I could see why Bass Strait has such a bad reputation for its weather. This was crazy – but the chopper was here and everyone had been lined up in single file and we were heading out to board no matter how windy it was.

Once we had boarded and the doors were closed you could feel the force of the wind buffeting the chopper as the pilots prepared it for takeoff. As the aircraft started to lift off the deck I couldn't help but smile at the thought of the old saying "bend over and kiss your arse goodbye", because that's exactly what it felt like we should all be doing. Once we were airborne the wind resistance didn't feel nearly as bad but the sight of the endless sea of whitecaps reminded me that it was still foul weather to be flying in. The chopper landed at Longford airport and we disembarked while they took on fuel. I've never been so glad to get my feet on solid ground.

After completing the second 2-week hitch on the Ocean Patriot, I returned home for a 2-week break. I was then sent to another rig in Bass Strait that was drilling in the offshore Otway Basin.

I flew to Melbourne again and caught another chopper from Essendon airport but this time we headed west and flew at low level all the way across the western suburbs and then followed the Victorian coastline along the Great Ocean Road until we headed out to sea once we got closer to the rig. It was an amazingly scenic flight and was much more interesting than the usual 2 hours over nothing but water, like I was used to in the North Sea and the Timor Sea.

The rig I was flying to was another Maersk jack-up rig, the Maersk Guardian, and the operating company was

Woodside Petroleum Ltd.

The well was Thylacine South-1 and it was being drilled from the Thylacine-A platform within the Tasmanian sector of the offshore Otway Basin, 70 km (43 mi) south of Port Campbell, Victoria. Thylacine South-1 was drilled to test a previously unproven gas pool in Units 1 and 2 (Thylacine Sandstone Member) in a down-faulted structural nose south of the main Thylacine horst. Secondary objectives included units within the Flaxman Formation and the deeper Upper Waarre Formation.

The Maersk Guardian was a much older rig than the Maersk Inspirer that I'd been on in the North Sea and while the accommodation was nowhere nearly as spacious, it was comfortable enough. There was a decent-sized gym with a room for cardio machines and a room for weight training, an indoor badminton court and even a solarium. I think the solarium must have been a relict from when the rig was originally drilling in the Norwegian sector of the North Sea – but it worked. The galley was spacious and the food was good – although it was unfair to compare it with the Ocean Patriot because their food was so exceptionally good that my food rating scale had now been calibrated to a very high standard for all rigs that I'd ever work on in the future.

When I first arrived on the rig, a rig I had never been on before and not expecting to know anyone on board, I was surprised when the first person I came across in the corridor was the safety coordinator, Peter Fitzgerald, who just happened to be one of the mine safety personnel at Osborne Mine when I worked there. We both had a little chuckle at the random encounter and how it proved what a small industry we really work in. It's always fun catching up with people you've worked with on other jobs, to lend an air of familiarity to your otherwise isolated workplace.

Thylacine South-1 encountered gas and condensate in both the primary and secondary objectives and would be plugged and suspended after wireline operations were completed.

With my two-week hitch completed I was ready to fly back home to Humpty Doo but it was a bittersweet fly-out day because it was going go be my last. My friend who had been babysitting for me was moving back to Mt Isa to live so I no longer had anyone to help me out at home so I now had to stay home and look for a "normal" job. I loved working offshore and the travel my job afforded me, and especially the people I worked with. I had no idea what I would do for a job but just hoped I'd find something. After working away for over seven years it was hard to imagine having to stay at home now and "settle down", but I had no choice for now.

****

While working offshore I had still been doing the odd aerobics class at the local gym when I was home on break and had still been participating in fitness industry training whenever possible. The industry had now done away with the old "Fitness Leader" qualification and introduced a new "Certificate III and IV in Fitness". To be a qualified personal trainer you needed to have completed the Certificate IV, which I had done in 2005 after undertaking a correspondence course. I was now fully accredited and registered as a personal trainer, gym instructor and group exercise instructor with Fitness Australia, the governing body for the fitness industry in Australia.

While I was looking for a geology job I saw a job advertised for a gym instructor at a soon-to-open new fitness centre franchise called "Curves" so I applied for a job there just in case it took me a while to find another geology job.

Curves was a ladies-only fitness centre where members participated in a circuit-style class that was coordinated by an instructor whose job it was to motivate and encourage the women as they moved around the circuit from one machine to the next. It was pretty tame compared to the type of training I would normally do myself but it was fun, and gave me something to do while I was job-hunting. When I instruct a traditional old-fashioned aerobics class I tended to yell like a drill sergeant to keep the participants motivated and fired up so it came as a bit of a shock to me when the manager of the Curves centre told me one day that she'd had a complaint about me from one of the members. It seems she didn't appreciate being yelled at and considered it rude of me to communicate with the members in that way. Boy, she sure wouldn't have wanted to be in any of my aerobics classes with me yelling at her to keep her lazy arse moving! Needless to say I didn't really fit into the Curves scene.

Within a several weeks I had found and started a new job as a project geologist for Compass Resources NL, working from their exploration office at Batchelor, NT. I was extremely lucky to find a geology job close enough to home that I could drive home each night, which meant I didn't need a babysitter. It wasn't offshore work but it meant I could still keep my career alive *and* be home for the kids every night. I was sure the geology gods were smiling down on me and I was eternally grateful to them!

Chapter 13

2006 – 2008

BROWNS OXIDE PROJECT

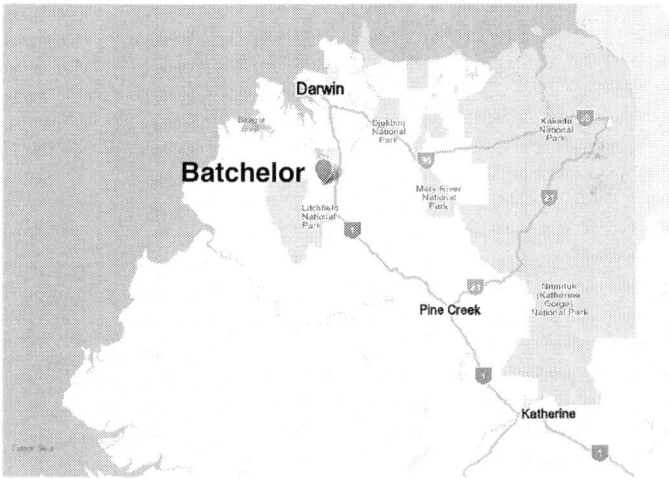

The Browns Oxide Project was a program being undertaken by Compass Resources NL in the lead up to the mining of the Browns polymetallic ore deposit, located near Batchelor, 98 km (61 mi) south of Darwin in the Northern Territory. Compass held 51 tenements covering an area of 250 km² surrounding the Rum Jungle mineral field.

The Browns deposit consists of a deposit of lead-zinc-copper-nickel-cobalt mineralisation, with some poorly defined zones of uranium. It has a quoted JORC resource of 84 million tonnes of ore hosted in four separate zones;

Browns, Browns East, Area 55 and Mount Fitch. The resources are subdivided into *oxide* and *sulfide* resources. The oxide resources consist of supergene or weathered sulfide ore where the ore mineralogy is dominated by metal oxides, hydroxides, clays and carbonates after the original sulfide mineralogy. The Browns sulphide resource is hosted beneath the supergene and oxide zones and has been defined down to a depth of -400m RL, and sits along a 2.5km strike. There are distinct zones of lead, zinc and copper enrichment, with consistent distribution of cobalt and nickel throughout the resource.

****

In 2006 the Stuart Highway in the Northern Territory still had an open speed limit but on the 1st January 2007 a speed limit of 130 km/hour (81 mph) was introduced. The drive from my Humpty Doo rural home to the Compass office in Batchelor was 68 km (42 mi) and took me about 50 minutes travelling at the allowed 130 km/hr. With the Browns Oxide Project starting up construction of a minesite and processing plant, there was now a lot more traffic on the stretch of road between Batchelor and Darwin.

When I first started working for Compass I was put on a 14-day on, 7-day off roster, cross-shifting with another geologist who was working FIFO out of Perth. The senior geologist was also working a two-week on, one week off rotation out of Perth so I was the only geologist in the office who lived locally. Within a few months I changed to working five days a week, Monday to Friday. For the first time in several years I was only required to work a 10-hour day, but not living at my workplace meant that I had nearly an hours drive every morning and afternoon getting to and from work so I was really working a 12-hr day anyway.

Compass were doing an extensive drilling program in all of their four mineralised zones at Browns, Browns East, Area 55 and Mount Fitch to prove up the resource for the oxide mine, and also investigate the extent of mineralisation in the deeper sulphide zone at Browns. The holes at Mount Fitch and Browns East were logged with a gamma ray tool after they had been drilled, to record any uranium oxide mineralisation present. A mobile unit was carried in the back of the work vehicle and the tool was lowered down the drillhole with a small winch. In 2006, Compass Resources reported resources of 4050 tonnes U3O8 at Mount Fitch.

The geology team was soon joined by another female geologist, Rachael, who was working FIFO out of Sydney to start off with but then relocated to Darwin. With the start of construction of the minesite offices and processing plant out at the Browns site, there was a lot of activity in the little town. Rachael and I shared the rig supervision duties and logging of the diamond drill core and reverse circulation (RC) samples.

Delays in the start-up of the Browns Mine meant the Turkish mine geologist, Koray, was able to help us out for a while also.

It was strange working back in Batchelor after having lived there several years before. There were quite a few locals who I remembered but the town certainly had a lot more activity in it than when we were living there. With the construction of the mine, came more professionals to the area, like geologists and engineers, so the town was no longer the sleepy little place it once was. With the influx of people came the inevitable increase in the cost of housing in the area. Old houses that used to rent for about $150 per week, were now demanding prices of up to $500 per week – that's if you could even find one!

The Gaden Drilling yard had closed up and was abandoned, with relics of some old drilling equipment lying around the yard. Looking at it made me feel like it was a lifetime ago since Gary had worked there.

Compass Resources sought the joint venture partnership of Hunan Nonferrous Metals Corporation, a Chinese government company; to help develop the Browns base metals mine but cost escalation and construction delays saw the project getting further and further delayed. *(The Global Financial Crises would eventually see the project grind to a halt and Compass Resources NL was placed in voluntary administration in 2009)*

In early 2008, my son Alex made a move to the Gold Coast with his girlfriend. While I was down on a visit helping them get settled over a couple of weekends I decided it was time I got out of Darwin too. Originally coming from Melbourne's inner suburbs, I was still definitely a city person at heart and although the years we had spent living in northern Australia's rural and regional areas was a great experience, I was ready to get back to civilization. I only had Becky at home with me now and we had recently downsized and moved into an apartment in Palmerston, so I no longer had the headache of looking after a 5-acre rural property.

I contacted a geologist friend, Justin, who had been the senior mine geologist at Osborne Mine when I worked there and was now working at the neighboring mine, Cannington, to see if he knew of any FIFO geology jobs in Queensland. He said they were looking for project geologists for a feasibility drilling program they were just starting and that I should apply for the job. Although it had already started, it was due to ramp up in the months to follow and they would need more geologists. With him being the senior geologist overseeing the drilling program I was practically guaranteed of getting the position. I gave it a lot of thought and I couldn't resist the chance to work with not only Justin again, but also two other geologists who I worked with at Osborne, Alan and Marcus. So after quite a few phone calls the decision was made – I was moving back to Queensland!

I gave four weeks notice at Compass and after a gathering of the troops at a local watering hole it was "adios!" to Batchelor and the Northern Territory for me.

Chapter 14

2008 - 2009

CANNINGTON MINE, QLD

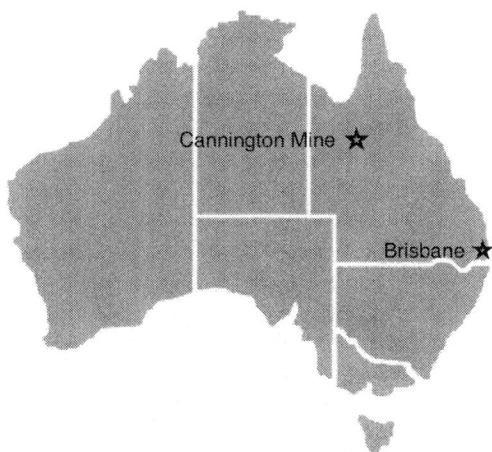

The Cannington silver-lead-zinc mine is an underground mine located in northwest Queensland, about 200 km (124 mi) southeast of Mount Isa. The deposit was discovered by BHP in 1990. Full production began in early 1999, and as of 2010 it was the largest and lowest cost silver and lead mine in the world. The major ore minerals are galena and sphalerite with silver occurring mainly as freibergite but is also present in solid solution within the galena.

The deposit is in Paleoproterozoic to Mesoproterozioc (2500–1000 mya) metamorphosed sedimentary rocks of the "Soldier's Cap Group", and is overlain by approximately 60 metres (197 ft) of Cretaceous and more recent overburden. The deposit was discovered as a result of an aeromagnetic survey of the Soldiers Cap Group in the eastern Mount Isa inlier. The area was selected for survey based upon extrapolations from known prospects and associated lithostratigraphy. The aeromagnetic survey pinpointed Cannington as a potential site and subsequent drilling proved it out. There is no surface expression of the mineralisation and the mine lies on a featureless semi-desert plain covered in sparse vegetation.

Up until the month I started at Cannington the mine flights only departed from Townsville, but during 2008 there was a skills shortage within the mining industry and they needed to attract more professional people to the operation, so they started doing flights from Brisbane directly to the minesite. The mine has a solely FIFO workforce due to its isolation.

Most of the workforce lived in Townsville so the majority of the flights departed from Townsville, with flights from Brisbane two days per week. The majority of the staff worked a 9-days on, 5-days off rotation, but I was employed on a 2-weeks on, 1-week off roster, flying in and out of Brisbane.

After settling into an apartment on the Gold Coast, I completed all the pre-employment medicals for BHP Billiton before heading out for my first hitch at the minesite. I was really excited to be working with Justin, Al, and Marcus again after spending over 4 years working with them at Osborne.

At the time, Cannington Mine was well known in the northwest Queensland mining community as having the best camp of all the FIFO mines in the area. The gym was as well-equipped as any city gym and as well as an outdoor swimming pool there was also a full size football oval in front of the dining mess and bar. The small patch of green grass on the oval was like an oasis amidst the surrounding semi-desert landscape.

The accommodation huts were very similar to those at Osborne Mine, and were self-contained rooms containing a single bed, wardrobe, study desk and ensuite bathroom. Originally everybody had their own dedicated room but over time, the workforce grew and the accommodation couldn't keep up with the numbers so many people had to share a room with someone who worked directly opposite them while they were on break. You were able to lock your work clothes in your wardrobe while you were off site so it wasn't much of an inconvenience having to share your room with your back-to-back.

The shifts were 12-hours long, from 6am to 6pm, and all work clothes had to be left in the change rooms at the minesite, due to health and safety regulations surrounding working at a lead mine. Laundry staff washed all the work clothes and returned them to your named box in the change room. Most people had their names embroidered on their clothes so the laundry staff knew where to return them.

While the men's change rooms contained communal showers, the ladies had separate shower cubicles to shower in. I was amused to find out one day that some of the male workers assumed the women showered in shared communal showers also and I shattered one man's fantasies by breaking the news to him that we didn't all shower together and lather each other up with soap like he probably imagined. I'm sure he probably still kept the dream alive anyway.

Like Mount Isa, Cannington experienced extremes in temperatures from 0°C (32°F) in winter, to 45°C (113°F) in summer, and the landscape could also be transformed from its regular arid desert to a monsoonal flood plain overnight, although heavy rain events were few and far between.

There was a 3 km sealed road that separated the minesite from the accommodation village, which also had a newly sealed running/walking track alongside it, complete with solar-powered lights. While there were buses that transported people to work and back, many people chose the healthy option and walked or jogged to, or from work.

A couple of months after I arrived on the Gold Coast there was a running festival weekend for the Gold Coast Marathon. The apartment I was living in was only 100 m from the start line so I decided to enter the 10 km event and be part of the festivities. The sight of all the marathon runners on the weekend must have inspired me because soon after that weekend I decided to start training for a marathon. After seeing an ad in the inflight magazine on the plane coming home from work one day, I decided to register for the London Marathon in 2009 and enter as a charity runner and raise funds for the Australian Heart Foundation.

I set a shorter term goal of running a half marathon in Melbourne in October 2008 and then build my training up gradually so I was ready for the full marathon in London by the following April. I was still really a 5 km jogger so had a long way to go.

While I was at work, I would run along the track at 4am before work, using a headlamp as extra security to make sure I would be able to see any snakes on the track. After work I'd go to the gym and do weight training before having dinner and going to bed.

By October I had increased my long run up to 21 km (13 mi) and was ready for the Melbourne half marathon, which I managed to complete in less than 2 hours. All I could think of when I crossed the finish line was: "how was I ever going to be able to run twice that distance in a marathon?!"

After committing to the fundraising there was no turning back – I had to accomplish the goal.

****

In October of 2008, Cannington's Life Extension Program had just committed to increasing the number of rigs we were going to need for "Project Silver Lining" – the study being undertaken to investigate the feasibility of progressively converting part of the current underground mining operation to an open cut mining operation, which could increase the mine life by an expected four years. The drilling campaign was ramping up to an expected five surface diamond rigs and an intense infill drilling program…and then the fallout from the Global Financial Crisis hit and the price for lead and silver plummeted in the second half of 2008. By January 2009 Project Silver Lining was all but dead. We struggled to keep drilling with two drilling rigs, while company lawyers for both BHP Billiton and the drilling contractors fought over a settlement for folding up the campaign.

As the backlog of core dwindled, so did the numbers of contract geologists and associated coreshed technicians. We had a fantastic crew working to process the thousands of metres of core that had been drilled and it was heartbreaking to see the plug get pulled on the project that, only a few months ago, promised to keep us all in work for at least a couple of years.

At all minesites I've worked at, the mining engineers, geotechnical engineers, mine geologists, and surveyors have all worked out of the same building so it becomes a very tight-knitted group of professionals all relying on each other to get their own job done. Working at a FIFO job probably teaches you to be more tolerant of different personalities because we're all stuck in this remote place together so we may as well make the most of it. The pool of talent and experiences that a workplace like this can pull together is remarkable and the more you find out about the lives of people you work with, the more interested you become in working with these people and making a difference to the outcomes of the project. Take for example, mine geologist Tanya – Tanya was working part-time at the mine when I first started at Cannington, and in the last year of her geology degree at James Cook University in Townsville. Once she graduated, she was put on full time as a graduate mine geologist and we worked out of the same office. Through chatting with her while doubled over cross-sections or entering drillhole data into the database I got to learn that this 6 foot tall blonde was not only a rock lover too but also rode a Ducati and spoke fluent Chinese, Russian and Portuguese, and dabbled in a few other languages *and* used to be a skydiver until she had a parachute malfunction and crash-landed and broke her neck...and she was still only in her early twenties! All of a sudden I felt like I had wasted decades of my life doing boring mundane things with only the English language to communicate in.

Tanya did a great job of being my publicity manager at Cannington while helping me raise funds for my London Marathon attempt. Together with coreshed technician and qualified photographer Nim, whom did a photo shoot of me training on the lonely stretch of outback road at the minesite for my web page, we hit the fundraising trail. My fundraising effort was bolstered by the fact that BHP Billiton had a charity matching policy whereby they would match any funds you raised for charity and contribute that same amount at the end of your fund-raising campaign. I managed to raise $5,500 and with BHP's contribution I was able to hand over $11,000 to the Heart Foundation on the completion of the London Marathon in April 2009.

While working at Cannington I was able to get sponsorship for the application for a membership with the Australasian Institute of Mining and Metallurgy (AusIMM). The AusIMM was founded in 1893 and provides services to professionals engaged in all facets of the global minerals sector. With a focus on providing leadership and opportunities to minerals industry professionals, The AusIMM delivers an ongoing program of professional development services to ensure members are supported throughout their careers, enabling them to provide high-quality professional input to industry and the community. The AusIMM represents more than 13,500 members drawn from all sections of the industry and supported by a network of branches and societies in Australasia and internationally.

To become a member you are required to have a relevant tertiary degree, a minimum of three years of relevant experience, and have the sponsorship of three Members or Fellows of The AusIMM. With the depth of experience within the geology and engineering departments at Cannington it was a good opportunity to gain sponsorship through the many AusIMM members who worked out of the same office as I did. The application process is quite involved and lengthy so I was excited when I finally became an official member of the AusIMM.

With BHP Billiton being the "worlds biggest miner" it came as no surprise that Cannington had a very comprehensive safety training program. When I look back on all the training courses I did while at Cannington it makes me wonder how I ever had time to get any work done in-between all the courses!

Qualification Name	Date Acquired
Authorised Permit Holder	2/03/09
Authorised Permit Issuer	2/03/09
Supervisor Appointment	6/10/08
Induction - Cannington Site Surface	13/06/08
Induction - Cannington Site Underground	13/06/08
Induction - Metalliferous Generic Core	10/06/08
Induction - Metalliferous Generic U/G	11/06/08
Toyota Vehicle Familiarisation	24/06/08
Better Attitude Towards Safety	14/06/08
CPR	13/06/08
Fatigue Management	15/06/09
Fire Extinguisher	11/06/08
Job Safety Analysis	10/07/08
Minearc Refuge Chamber	13/06/08
Permit Issuer Competency	22/02/09
Permit to Work Holder Competency	22/02/09
QMS123	21/08/08
Safe Behaviour Observation	24/07/08
Self Rescuer / EBA 6.5	13/06/08
Self Rescuer Savox MSA	13/06/08
Take Five	13/06/08
Code of Business Conduct	27/05/09
Harassment and Discrimination	25/06/08
GSAP Purchasing Fundamentals	11/08/08
Basic First Aid (HLTFA1A or MNMG204A)	12/06/08
Light Vehicle Operation- S/face	24/06/08
Ground Awareness	14/06/09

Although I was technically a contractor employed for a particular project, I was employed as a BHP Billiton employee, which meant when the project came to an end in June 2009 I received a redundancy payout. Because of the downturn in mineral prices, the entire minesite experienced personnel losses in an attempt to reduce the costs of running the mine. I knew I would definitely be going because the drilling program got shut down but many of the other minesite personnel were left in limbo not knowing who was going and who would stay. It was a tense and unpleasant time and really affected the morale of the workforce. Like many millions of people worldwide, I became a statistic of the "GFC" so it was time to look for another job and say goodbye to my old, and new, friends at Cannington.

Chapter 15

2009 – 2010

COAL SEAM GAS, QLD

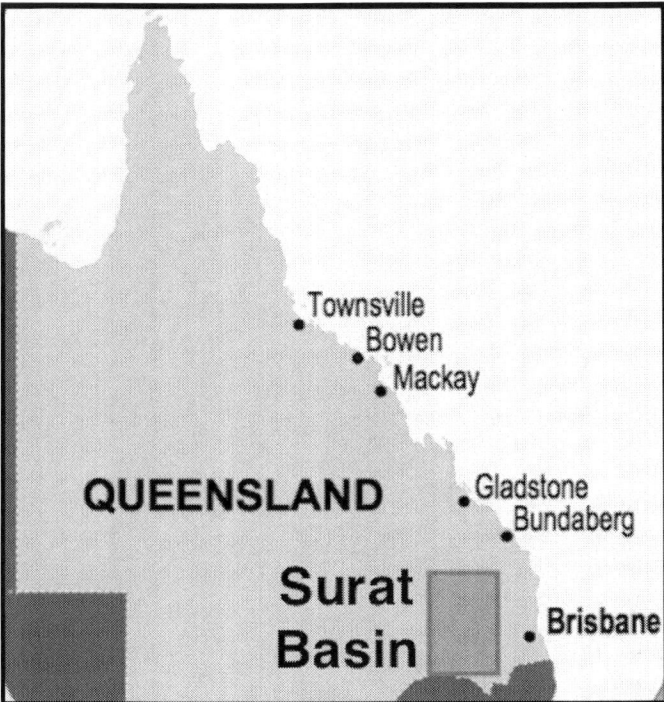

With my job at Cannington coming to an end, I had to start looking around for something else. Despite the downturn in the minerals industry, the then-fledgling coal seam gas industry was gaining momentum and I knew there was a lot of drilling taking place in the Surat and

Bowen basins because my son had been working on drilling rigs in the region for a few years now.

When I had been working as a mudlogger in the Timor Sea a few years earlier, I had worked with another Sperry mudlogger Brent, who was a petroleum geologist, and he later went on to become an operations geologist for Queensland Gas Company (QGC). Every now and again he'd drop me a line and ask if I was interested in working as a wellsite geologist in the Surat Basin because they had quite an extensive drilling program underway and were looking for wellsite geologists. Each time he contacted me I was already employed and happy where I was so I declined his offer, but now I was hoping the opportunity was still available.

Brent and I met up over a few beers at a restaurant in the Queens St Mall in Brisbane one evening and discussed the details of the job and within a few weeks I had an official offer of employment from QGC working as a wellsite geologist in their southeast Queensland coal seam gas fields.

The job was a "drive in – drive out" position from my home base on the Gold Coast and I would be working a 2-week on/2-week off rotation. I needed to provide my own work vehicle, which had to be a four-wheel-drive, so I used the money I received from my redundancy package at Cannington to buy a new utility work car. I thought of more indulgent things to spend that money on other than a Triton Ute but a secure job was more important now so I had to do what I needed to get started in a few weeks time.

****

Coal seam gas (CSG) is primarily methane and is found in coal deposits. The "natural gas" collects in underground coal seams by bonding to the surface of coal particles. The coal seams are generally filled with water and it's the pressure of the water that keeps the gas as a thin film on the surface of the coal.

The large Early Jurassic to Early Cretaceous Surat Basin occupies 300,000 km² of central southern Queensland and central northern New South Wales. It has a maximum sediment thickness of 2,500 m and deposition was relatively continuous and widespread.

The coal seam gas in the Surat Basin is contained within the Walloon Coal Measures subgroup, which is approximately 300 metres thick. The Wallooon is unconformably overlain by the Springbok Sandstone and contains interbedded coal seams within the three distinct units of the Juandah Coal Measures, the Tangalooma Sandstone and the Taroom Coal Measures.

CSG has been produced from the Surat Basin since 1996 for the domestic gas market, and further exploration since then has revealed the extent of the resource. Current fields are being expanded and new gas fields developed to meet the domestic gas demand and the demand created by the LNG projects that are being undertaken by QGC (BG-Group-Shell), Arrow Energy, Origin Energy and Santos.

****

Never having worked in the coal or coal seam gas industry before, I decided to do a 3-day "Coal Seam Gas Reservoir Assessment" course through the Runge Group training providers. The course covered the basics of coal geology, gas reservoir geology, determining net coal, gas in place and gas deliverability, and an applications overview for using the acquired data in a coal mining environment. Not only did I learn a lot but also it gave me a boost in confidence before starting a new job that was a bit out of my previous experience field. The data collection aspect of the job would be no different to what I had previously done while mudlogging offshore but it was comforting to know a bit more about coal geology and methane gas storage after the course. The cost of the course was tax deductible so I tried to focus on that rather than the three thousand dollars I was out of pocket for doing it. Sometimes you just have to spend money to make money, as they say. I've always been happy to spend money on training courses out of my own pocket, whether it's for geology or for the fitness industry – up-skilling can't always be done on the job, especially when you're a contractor.

****

With my new Triton and sample sieves I headed off down the Warrego Highway to my first hitch with QGC. Queensland Gas Company had been taken over by BG Group in November of 2008 but the coal seam gas operations in the Surat Basin still operated under the QGC banner. QGC was already operating the Argyle, Argyle East, Bellevue, Berwyndale, Berwyndale South, Codie/Lauren, Kenya, Kenya East and Woleebee gas fields and I would be involved in the development drilling campaign around these fields that would eventually form the upstream network of wells that would feed the LNG plant being built at Curtis Island in Gladstone.

I spent my first 2-week hitch shadowing another wellsite geologist to learn what was involved in the job and then from my second hitch I was on my own. The drilling rigs were a stand-alone operation from the production fields and as such, the drilling crew stayed in a mobile camp that was positioned within a short drive of the well site. The camp was just like I lived in years ago in the demountable dongas of the Rockdril camps – minus the alcohol and drugs. During one hitch there was even a security team that came in with sniffer dogs and searched all the rooms in the camp and on the rig for contraband. Someone lost his job that day. The times had certainly changed from when you could party hard the night before then rock up for work the next day. Health and safety regulations, and the strict enforcement of them, were now strongly entrenched in the resources sector and if you didn't want to abide by them then you were working in the wrong industry.

During the two weeks of my hitch, I worked and lived out of an office at the drill site. I also had a room at the camp but with the drilling being a 24-hour operation and me being the only geologist, I was required to remain at the rig most of the time. I would drive back to the camp for meals and a shower because there were no bathroom facilities at the rig, except for a port-a-loo.

Having to be on-call and at the rig 24-hours a day meant it was practically impossible to do any training. The only time I could risk being un-contactable while out running was if the rig was moving location and there was no drilling being done. There was no gym to train in so I couldn't do any weight training either. I just had to wait till I got home.

Part of the daily requirements of the job were a morning and afternoon update phone call to the operations geologist in the Brisbane office but it was impossible to get mobile coverage at the rig sites with a normal mobile phone. I had to spend a thousand dollars on a Telstra "Farmers Phone" and also get an antenna hard-wired into my car to give me any chance of getting a phone signal. Despite only being 200 km from a capital city, and only about 50 km from the regional centre of Dalby, the pathetically inadequate telecommunications system that the monopoly of Telstra provides in Australia is less than third world standards. So even with my super-expensive mobile phone and flash-looking antenna I was still having to find high ground and stand on top of my car to get my morning call done some days.

The local community in the Surat Basin was divided in the support for the burgeoning Coal Seam Gas industry in their backyards. There were pockets of areas where hostility towards people working in the industry resulted in physical attacks and while these were isolated incidents, everyone was advised to remain vigilant at all times. In hindsight it was probably a bad idea that I had issued my new car with the number plates 000 CSG as this, along with the "QGC" company logo magnets that we were supposed to have fixed to our vehicle doors, were a dead give away that I was one of "them". Whenever I had to drive through the small community that was best known for its hostility towards the industry, I would pullover a few kilometres out of town and take off the QGC door magnets in the hope I could sneak through town without being recognized.

The best feature of my new car was, without a doubt, the stainless steel nudge bar grille guard that would hopefully provide a safety barrier between the front-end of my car and the many kangaroos on the roads I travelled on between well sites. I was eventually able to confirm its effectiveness after an encounter with a large kangaroo late one afternoon while driving back to the camp. I was sitting on the speed limit of 100 km/hour when the roo appeared from the side of the road and ran straight out in front of me. As it hit the nudge bar it was effortlessly bounced off the front of my car and flung to the side of the road, barely even registering a thump from inside the car. I immediately pulled over to the side of the road and went looking for the roo but it was nowhere to be seen so I guess it was still alive after bouncing off the car. The front of my car showed no visible sign of the kangaroo having hit it – yay, no insurance claim necessary! Effectiveness proven.

****

The monitoring of the drilling operations was done by an external third-party company called "PASON", who provided a system of sensors for monitoring the basic drilling parameters. It was a simple user-friendly system of obtaining and viewing real time drilling data and downloading of LAS files to send to the office.

All of our reporting and data acquisition was done via the Gravitas operational geology software suite which was very comprehensive and provided shared access to all the well data and drilling data with the Brisbane office.

At the completion of drilling, wireline logs were run to obtain gamma ray, density, caliper, neutron and sonic data. These logging runs had to be witnessed by the wellsite geologist.

With the drilling being very fast most of the time, sleep deprivation was an accepted part of the job. Red Bull was your friend. You managed it the best you could and always came through with the deliverables at reporting time, no matter what.

****

Now that I was working back in the Oil and Gas industry I wanted to do some further study on petroleum geology because my original geology degree was steered towards minerals geology rather than petroleum geology, so I started a correspondence post graduate Petroleum Geology course through the University of New South Wales. Only working two weeks on - two weeks off, meant I had a lot of time at home to study on my breaks so I managed to complete the course, along with practical assignments and exams over a three month period. I was another $2,200 out of pocket but was feeling all the more knowledgeable for it.

After completing this course I got the bug for wanting to work offshore again but as a wellsite geologist this time, not a mudlogger. Despite the exorbitant cost of the oil and gas industry courses, I really needed to gain more knowledge so I sacrificed another $12,000 to fly to Dubai for two weeks and complete two 5-day courses on "Operations Geology" and "Well Log Interpretation". I was the only person in the courses who had paid for the course out of their own pocket as everyone else was sent there by their employers – no such privilege for me, being a contractor.

The courses were quite intense but very interesting and it was also fun networking with other people in the industry who came from completely different backgrounds to me. Most of the course participants were from Middle

Eastern countries and worked for some of the world's biggest oil companies. It was great exploring Dubai in the time between courses and I even got to experience a desert safari with a couple of other ladies from the course, Susana and Joanna. I now know that I get carsick from driving over sand dunes at high speed!

****

Once I got back to Australia I booked to re-do my Sea Survival (TBOSIET) course, which had expired since I had last done it in Aberdeen in 2005. If I was going to get the chance to go back offshore then I wanted to be ready to fly at short notice. That was another thousand-dollar investment in my career for which I was hoping I would eventually see a return on my investment.

After my years of working as a mudlogger offshore I now had quite a few contacts in the offshore oil and gas industry so thought I'd try and see if I could get work as a wellsite geologist offshore. I contacted my mudlogging mate Dan (who I ran the Dili 10km fun run with), who was now working as a wellsite geologist offshore, and asked him for advice on getting a start offshore. He suggested I send my CV to the recruitment agency he was working through at the time, so I did that and kept my fingers crossed something might come up.

After a couple of months, while I was home on break, I just happened to be messaging Dan and he mentioned that the manager of the recruitment agency was in Brisbane for the APPEA (Australian Petroleum Production and Exploration Association) annual conference being held at the convention centre. Keen for a chance to meet with this person face-to-face I sent Ted a message saying that I'd love to catch up for a chat if he had the time while he was in Brisbane. I was excited to get a reply soon after saying that he'd be happy to catch up at the convention centre after the day's sessions had finished. We arranged a time and I drove from the Gold Coast to Brisbane and met with him, as the conference was finishing for the week.

There were post-conference drinks for all the conference delegates down at Southbank, in front of the convention centre, and I managed to get my way in using someone else's nametag that wasn't able to stay for the drinks. The opportunity to network with industry people was invaluable and Ted introduced me to some other people who were involved in the industry. I was hoping this could be the chance I had been waiting for.

For several weeks there was no news from Ted although he did seem confident of getting me a job eventually and I knew he was trying hard to find something. Then finally he rang me with good news that he had secured an onshore job for me in the Cooper Basin. While it wasn't offshore work, I was happy to get the start and just hoped it would give me more experience and lead onto something offshore eventually.

I gave QGC four weeks notice of resignation and looked forward to another change in my career – hopefully one that would see me working back offshore as a wellsite geologist in the not-too-distant future.

Chapter 16

2010

SOUTHERN COOPER BASIN

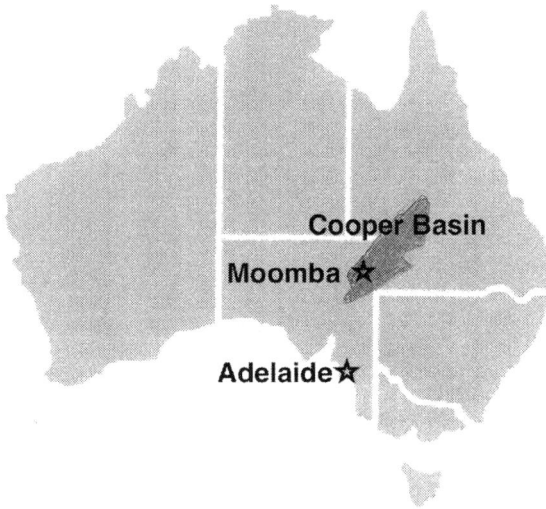

The Cooper Basin is located mainly in the southwest corner of Queensland and extends into northeastern South Australia. It contains the most important onshore petroleum and natural gas deposits in Australia, with the first commercial discovery of gas occurring in 1963. Pipelines transport gas to the major markets of Brisbane, Adelaide and Sydney.

The largest producer in the basin is Santos Limited with its main production facility at Moomba, in the far northeastern corner of South Australia.

All employees work on a fly in-fly out roster basis; there is no permanent resident population in Moomba. Moomba has a sealed airstrip and 'camp' accommodation for its FIFO residents who are, largely, Santos employees. Scheduled services are operated daily to and from Adelaide but members of the public are not able to fly to Moomba; only employees, contractors and authorised visitors are able to visit.

****

After flying from Brisbane to Adelaide I met up with a group of people who were also heading out to the rig I was going to be working on. We all caught the chartered flight to Moomba and were picked up in a "troop carrier" and driven out to the rig, which was getting ready to drill the well "Forge-1" for Strike Energy Limited.

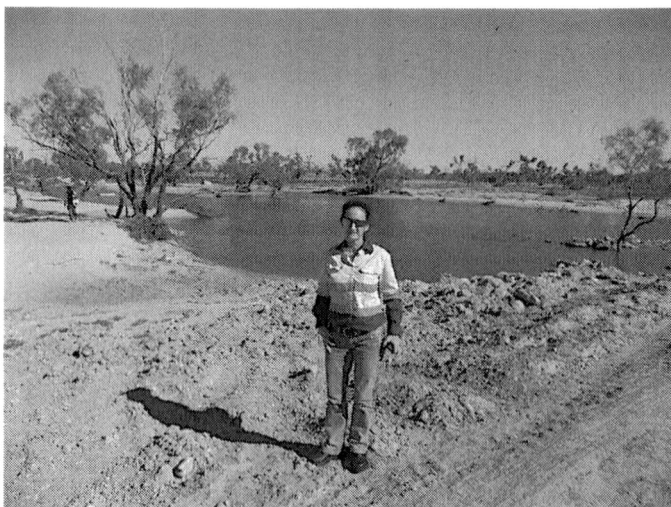

The wellsite was in a remote area of northeastern South Australia, in the Strzelecki Desert region on the southern fringe of the Cooper Basin. Once we left Moomba there were only sandy desert tracks to drive on, including a 120 km stretch of the Strzelecki Track.

Once we turned off the Strzelecki Track we had to drive 41 km along a sandy access road to the rig's location. As we were heading in a westerly direction it meant we were driving perpendicular to rows of parallel sand dunes that dominate the Strzelecki Desert. The sand ridges have a trend of SSE-NNW and continue parallel for kilometers. With a dune crest roughly every kilometre it was quite a rollercoaster drive to get to the rig.

When I left home I had no idea how long I'd be away, other than I would be out in the desert for as long as it took to drill the well. I was expecting to be gone for around four weeks but took enough toiletries to last longer, if need be. In regards to the clothes I packed, it didn't matter how long I would be gone because all I needed was one set of good clothes to wear on the flight to Adelaide, two sets of work clothes, and some running gear. It was the middle of winter and although we were in the desert, I knew it got very cold out there overnight, and even during the day sometimes, so I also packed a big fluorescent yellow work parka – and I was very glad I did. Minimum temperatures plummeted to near 0°C at times and if the wind picked up during the day it could stay freezing cold all day. My years of living and working in north west Queensland, and in remote drilling camps, wisened me up to just how cold the Australian outback can get. With minimums down to 0°C in winter and maximums of over 50°C in summer, central Australia has one of the most extreme ranges of climate anywhere in the world.

The camp was already set up when we arrived and was on the cleared lease area, about 150 metres from the rig. I was the only female in the camp of about 20 people, and had a room to myself with a shared bathroom. The blocks of sleeping quarters were quite new so they were as clean and comfortable as you could expect in a desert camp. Timber decking walkways between the rooms kept a lot of the sand out of your room although it was impossible to keep the sand out completely.

There was no gym in the camp so the only training I could hope to get would be a run down the sandy access track, but being the only geologist on site meant that I would be on-call 24 hours a day so I'd have to pick my times to go running when there wasn't any drilling going on. When I did go for a run I'd let the cook know, and write on the board in the mess what time I hoped to be back, so if I wasn't back in camp soon after that time then someone needed to come looking for me.

****

Once drilling began I managed my work time to get enough sleep early in the night so I could be in the mudlogging unit by 3 am each morning. I would log the samples that were drilled while I was sleeping so I could have a morning report prepared by 7 am each day.

Forge-1 was drilled to evaluate the coal seam gas potential of Tertiary, Cretaceous and Permian coals on a structural high in the Weena Trough, located on the southern margin of the Cooper Basin. The primary objective was to core the Permian aged Epsilon and Patchawarra Formation coals to determine their gas content. The secondary objective was to investigate the potential for coal development in the shallower Tertiary Eyre Formation and the Cretaceous Winton Formation.

The well was drilled to a total depth of 1,351 metres with total gas shows of up to 1.8% being encountered and a composite coal thickness of 24m being cored. Cement plugs were set and the well was suspended to enable future deepening and evaluation of the deeper Patchawarra coals.

After 4 weeks in the camp it was time to head back to Moomba and fly home but we were racing against the clock with the weather. Unseasonable rain events were already causing minor flooding on the access track into the wellsite. A group of us headed out in the troop carrier and fortunately made it through the flooded dips in-between the sand dunes by using one of the trucks to pull us through with a towrope. We were very relieved when we finally got to the Strzelecki Track, which was built up, higher than the surrounding ground and was compacted to a harder surface so the rain hadn't affected it as much. There were still slippery stretches along here and we didn't feel 100% confident of making the chartered flight until we finally hit the streets of Moomba. It was a nice feeling being on the plane and looking down at the rain-soaked desert below us knowing we got out before it was too late. Drill crew members would not be so lucky and were unable to demobilize the rig and it had to remain on site until months later when the roads had dried up. Unseasonable rains in the Lake Eyre catchment areas of northeast South Australia and southwest Queensland during 2009 and 2010 saw the highest run-off into Lake Eyre in over 30 years. We narrowly missed having to get evacuated off the site by helicopter.

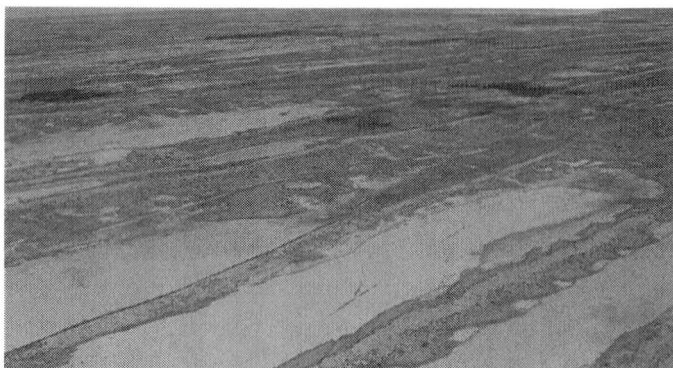

Chapter 17

2010

TIMOR SEA

After returning from the Cooper Basin, I had a few weeks at home before I got a call to say I had a hitch back offshore as a wellsite geologist. I was so excited to finally be given the chance to work offshore again and was fortunate to be heading back to familiar territory on the Ensco 104 in the Timor Sea.

ConocoPhillips were coming to the end of their most recent phase of development drilling at Bayu-Undan and as the campaign had extended for longer than originally expected they needed another geologist to fill in until the end. I don't think I've ever been so excited to be going back to work!

I flew from Brisbane to Darwin, where I stayed overnight, and then caught the Air North flight to Dili the next morning. It had been five years since my last hitch in the Timor Sea but it felt like only a few months ago once I got to the heliport in Dili and saw the same familiar faces of the logistics crew.

Paul Greystone and Lisa Paris were always happy to show us around Dili whenever we were spending time there on standby from the rig. They introduced me to the Dili Hash House Harriers and I joined them for a run around the streets of Dili and later for the post-run celebration drinks on more than one occasion during my last job on the Ensco 104. It was always fun spending time socializing in Dili and getting to know the ground logistics crew and helicopter pilots who we would normally have very little contact with.

After having our bags checked and then the helicopter briefing, we were led out to the chopper in single file and boarded the aircraft. It was great working back in the tropics and not having to wear the survival suit in the chopper. It was also great getting the chance to fly over the East Timor highlands again at low level in the helicopter. The trip to the rig takes us from the north of the half-island country, across the mountain range and over the south coast to the Timor Sea. It's an amazing flight and gives you a bird's eye view of the small island nation. Looking down over the rugged mountainous country it was hard to imagine the atrocities that took place there only a decade ago. The jungle below us would have been teaming with guerilla forces and militia and the innocent victims of the unspeakable brutality of the Indonesian military. It was still a third-world country, which were all the more incredible given that it was only a 50-minute flight from Darwin in northern Australia.

Once I was on the rig and the induction completed, I took my bags to my cabin. I couldn't believe how the accommodation had deteriorated in the 5 years since I had last been there. The rooms were very shabby and the ensuite bathroom had tiles missing from the floor and rust-stained walls and flooring. The good news was that I didn't have to share my bedroom or bathroom with anyone while I was off-tour so I was more than happy to sacrifice a clean bathroom for a private bathroom.

Once I had changed into my coveralls, I headed out to the mudlogging unit and caught up with the day-shift wellsite geologist, who just happened to be the Sperry data engineer who I worked with when I was last on the rig as a mudlogger. It was great to be working with Trevor again and he gave me a quick introduction to R-WEB and the things I'd need to know before starting the night shift at 6 pm. R-WEB, like Gravitas that I'd used when working for QGC, provides geological software tools that organize operational well data in a quality controlled database and is accessible by multiple users at any time without corrupting the original dataset. It was pretty easy to find my way around it, as it's quite intuitive and user-friendly. After a brief introduction to my duties I left to go and get a few hours sleep before having to go back on shift at 6 pm and then work through to 6 am.

When I passed through the men's change room (remember, there are no women's change rooms on this rig – just men's) I was surprised to see that one of the two toilets in the room had been converted to a "squat" toilet, an indication that the rig must have spent quite a bit of time working in Asia since I had last been on it. The toilets were just as bad as I remembered them, with pee all over the floor and toilet bowl. Why is it so hard for men to get it *in* the bowl? And don't even get me started on the skid marks! I was the only female on the rig of 120 people so piss-covered toilets with skid marks comes with the territory when you're a woman working in a man's world.

The well that was being drilled was the last in a series of horizontal gas production wells. Being a horizontal well meant that the cuttings descriptions were simplified because about half the well was being drilled through the one formation without much variation in the samples. This gave me the opportunity to spend more time getting used to R-WEB without the pressure of complicated sample descriptions to slow me down.

Once I found my feet with the job I started to get into a routine of training before starting my shift, with a jog on the helideck or workout in the gym. It was easy to slip into a routine in the familiar surroundings. A big change was the fact that the accommodation was now run by Indian catering contractors so all the main meals were Indian food, with an Australian choice for the Aussies. The Indian cuisine was excellent and there was a good choice of dishes and accompaniments.

The hitch came and went too fast and before I knew it I was back home and looking for another job.

Chapter 18

2010

KAGARA, NORTH QLD

After getting back from my hitch offshore in the Timor Sea, one month dragged into two and I still didn't have any sign of another contract offshore. After two months of no work I got a call from my friend at Cannington, Tanya, asking if I was interested in doing a project geologist job for Kagara Zinc in north Queensland.

Tanya's partner Mick, was a mining engineer working at Kagara's Surveyor mine in north Queensland and he heard they were looking for a contract geologist to help with the exploration drilling program that was being undertaken to investigate known near mine resources and explore other nearby areas that had shown significant resource growth potential. After contacting the senior exploration geologist who was working on the drilling campaign and expressing my interest in the job, I was asked if I could start the following week.

The South Surveyor 1 Mine was a copper, gold, lead, silver and zinc deposit on the banks of the Dry River in Queensland about 300 km west of Townsville. Kagara Zinc Ltd commenced mining at the Surveyor mine in 2003 and in 2010 they were conducting drilling to further explore the near-mine area.

The Surveyor mine had a FIFO workforce, as well as some workers who drove in from outlying areas. I flew from Brisbane to Townsville then caught the chartered mine flight out to the minesite the next morning. The small airstrip was only a few kilometres from the mine and camp and the plane was met by a troop carrier that drove us all to the accommodation where we'd be staying.

Both the mine and the accommodation were a lot smaller than any other place I'd ever worked or lived. The self-contained huts were spacious and clean and scattered in a random cluster on the side of an undulating hill. The short walk to my room passed an open-air gym with old rusty equipment, but it was still a gym, and while I continued to walk to my room I was already planning what kind of gym session I could do the next morning with the limited equipment available.

I changed into my work clothes and was escorted along the short walk to the Surveyor mine offices where I was met by the senior exploration geologist. There was a backlog of core at the exploration yard where another three contract geologists were already at work logging the core. The exploration yard was a beautiful tranquil setting on the edge of the river, with no noisy minesite traffic. There was a row of accommodation huts and a separate ablutions block, which catered for the exploration geologist and his full-time field assistants who had been working in this area for several years.

I was shown through the logging process and was surprised to see they were still recording their logging on paper sheets which then had to be entered into the computers in the office, which took almost as much time as it took to log the core in the first place. I hadn't logged onto paper sheets since I started my first job as a geologist with Western Mining in 1983 and was well aware of the time saved by logging directly onto a laptop computer. It only took me the first day on the job to get frustrated with the inefficient method of logging and the next day I took my own laptop out to the coreshed and logged directly onto that and later imported the excel file into the database, saving me a couple of hours at the end of the day not having to manually type in the logging I had done. That gave me two extra hours every day to log more core!

I did two 2-week hitches at Surveyor mine with a week break at home in-between. The last flight out of there at the end of October was in torrential rain with the pilot having virtually no visibility the whole way back to Townsville. It was only a small dual-propeller light aircraft that sat about 10 people and it was the most unpleasant flight I have ever been on. The plane was too small to be able to fly high enough to get over the tropical storm clouds so we had to fly straight through them. The small aircraft was being buffeted around by the turbulent conditions and I seriously feared for my life. I was sitting in the seat directly behind one of the pilots and I could see him texting on his mobile phone at one stage and I couldn't help but wonder if he was sending his wife a text to say he loved her in case he never got the chance to tell her in person again. I've never been happier to touch down at Townsville airport and get out of a plane!

After the two hitches there was no more core to log at Surveyor mine but before I left the site I was asked by the exploration geologist if I was interested in doing a couple of months work on a drilling program Kagara were doing up near their Mt Garnet minesite. I was more than happy to take any work I could get so agreed to do the job, which would keep me employed up until Christmas.

As there was only about 6 weeks of work I decided to drive my car up there and work straight through, just taking a couple of weekends off in between. Having my car up there meant that I could not only drive to Cairns on my weekends off but I could also carry some gym equipment up with me so I could train in my bedroom while I was up there. I knew I would be staying in a cabin at a local caravan park and there would be no gym close by.

crews – all a bit more relaxed than what I was used to.

I worked seven days a week although I took the weekend off a couple of times and drove to Cairns for a bit of a break. Workplace health and safety regulations don't look favourably upon you working for six weeks straight so I was happy to have a mini holiday in Cairns after 14 days at work in Mount Garnet.

The drilling program was completed on the 20th December, which meant I was again out of a job and not knowing what I'd be doing in the New Year. The Kagara exploration manager told me they planned to have another drilling program for the following year and that he'd be in touch with me over the next few weeks to discuss any work opportunities.

For the time being, I just wanted to drive home as quickly as I could because I had some of my kids and Gary all planning to be at my place on the Gold Coast for Christmas and the Queensland weather bureau was predicting flooding rain events over the next couple of days. I was driving from Mount Garnet in north Queensland, Christopher was to drive from a drilling job in central Queensland and Gary was driving from a job in western Queensland and we were all lucky enough to have made it back to the Gold Coast just before the worst of the storms hit. Within 24 hours of us all getting home, flooding rains forced the evacuation of thousands of people from towns and cities with at least 90 towns and over 200,000 people being affected. Three-quarters of the council areas within the state of Queensland were declared disaster zones. About 300 roads were closed, including nine major highways. During the flooding it was reported that more than three-quarters of Queensland was affected by flooding and over 40 people lost their lives. We were all so lucky to have made it home and to high ground before the worst of it hit. Normally all three of us would be working FIFO and not having to drive from jobs, but this was an exception that almost saw us all in the middle of a disaster zone.

Once we were all safely home it was time to relax and enjoy the Christmas break and not have to think about work – well, at least for a couple of weeks.

Chapter 19

2011 - 2012

XSTRATA, MOUNT ISA

In the first week of 2011 I received an email from my friends Roslyn and Steve Budd, who worked at Mount Isa Mines, alerting me to a job position being advertised for a project geologist at the mine. The position was for approximately one year, working on a drilling program for Xstrata's Black Star expansion project it had announced in 2010, which was dubbed the Black Star Open Cut 'Deeps' Project.

By this time I had already been advised by the exploration geologist at Kagara Zinc that there would be a further 12 months of work for me with them in the Mount Garnet region if I was interested, but I was curious about the Mount Isa role so emailed the senior geologist who had posted the ad to find out more about the position.

While I knew the Kagara job would be a lot more relaxed than working for the big miner Xstrata, I thought I really should challenge myself professionally so decided to apply for the Mount Isa job – and I got it!

The position was FIFO from Brisbane on a 2-week on, 1-week off roster but with my place of accommodation in Mount Isa being 5 kilometres away from the minesite office, I decided to drive my car up there on my first hitch and then leave it up there for the duration of the contract.

The 2,000 km (1,243 mi) drive from the Gold Coast to Mount Isa had me driving through the worst affected areas in the recent floods from only a few weeks before. While driving through the Lockyer Valley, west of Brisbane, the reality of the devastation was still evident in the washed-out sections of highway and debris-laden fence lines. It was eerie looking at it as I drove cautiously through the on-going roadwork teams that were gradually rebuilding the roads and clearing the rubbish. Only a few weeks before I had watched the live TV broadcasts of people being washed to their deaths from the top of cars and homes in this district and it felt surreal driving through the aftermath of it now.

Once I cleared the Great Dividing Range at Toowoomba the roads of the western plains weren't much better. For practically the entire 2,000 km journey I was dodging potholes on the highway where chunks of bitumen had been washed away in the heavy run-off from the rain events. And even more unusual was the fact that the country all the way from Brisbane to Mount Isa was covered in lush green grass – instead of the brown dusty plains they normally are. I had done this trip many times before and had never seen outback Queensland looking so green – or the highway looking so wrecked. Not only did I have to watch out for kangaroos now, but also very deep potholes that were hard to see until you were right on top of them. I was very glad to finally get to Mount Isa after driving for nearly two days, and I drove straight to my friend's place where I'd spend my first night back in "the Isa".

It had been six and a half years since we had lived in Mount Isa and it felt strange being back working there as a FIFO worker – especially when I had my car with me. It was like a hybrid FIFO roster – flying in and out but living in town like a local.

My contract included all travel expenses to Mount Isa and accommodation at the Parkside Apartments, where I had a two-bedroom apartment to myself. Driving my car up meant I was able to take some gym equipment with me so I was able to train in my room before work each day. I took with me an exercise bench, an E-Z curl bar, some weight plates and I later bought a chin-up bar that I mounted in the one of the doorways inside the apartment. I now had a fully functioning gym in my home-away-from-home.

Arriving for my first hitch in the middle of summer meant I could expect the temperature to reach 40 - 45°C (104 - 113°F) most days for the next couple of months at least. Fortunately the Parkside Apartments were air-conditioned, but unfortunately they were evaporative air-conditioners so as soon as there was any humidity you also got black mould growing all over your walls. I didn't miss that aspect of living in Mount Isa since we had moved away from there. Although the city normally had very hot and dry summers, they were affected by any monsoonal conditions during the northern "wet season" and could experience random high rainfall events. Of course rain in "the Isa" was always a welcomed event and seeing the Leichhardt River flooding the main streets into town was always a great source of entertainment for the locals.

Roslyn and Steve Budd were my only remaining geology friends who still lived in Mount Isa but two of my gym instructor friends who I used to work with at the Fitness Warehouse gym were locals of the town and still resided there. Lyn and Alison no longer worked at the gym but were still very active with sporting events in the local community. The gym had since relocated to new premises and was owned by different owner/managers so the fun place I used to work at, that was such a big part of my life when I used to live in Mount Isa, no longer existed as I knew it. I was soon to realise that once you leave a place, it never has the same feel when you return years later. That was especially true for a city like Mount Isa, which had a high turnover rate of professional people who lived and worked there.

When I had left Mount Isa in 1998, all the MIM operations were underground, including the copper mine, the lead mine and Hilton mine. In 2003, Xstrata purchased Mount Isa Mines and following the take-over, Xstrata split the Mount Isa operations into two separate streams: a copper stream and a lead-zinc-silver stream. The copper stream became part of Xstrata Copper and the lead-zinc-silver stream became part of Xstrata Zinc.

When the evaluation of the mineralisation first began in Mount Isa in 1924, the average width and grade of four ore zones was defined to the 24-metre level. These zones were known as Black Star, Mount Isa, Black Rock and Rio Grande. The underground mining of these zones saw the start of production at Mount Isa Mines.

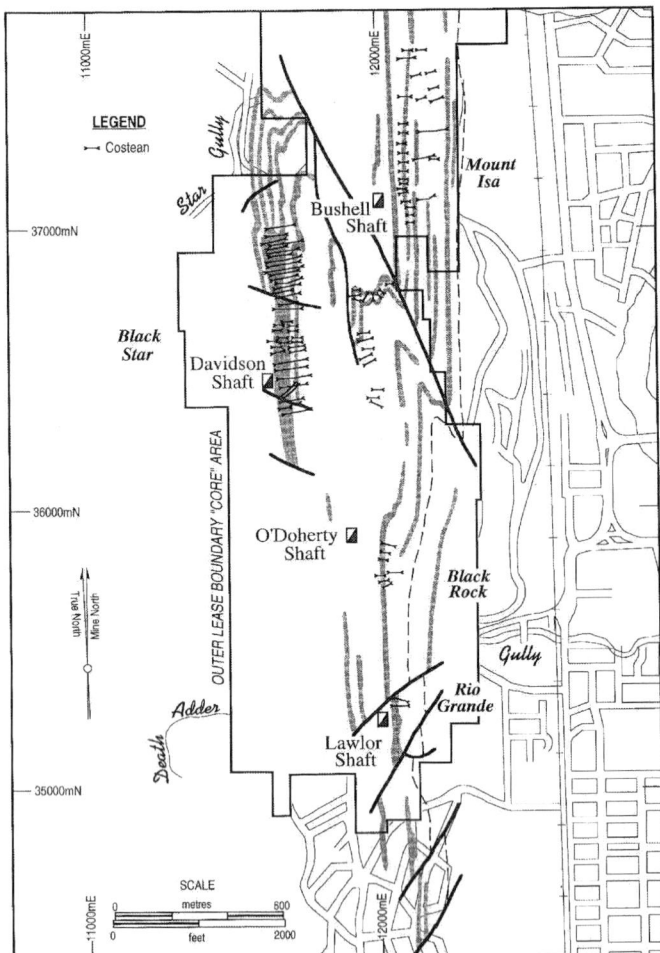

In 2004, as production from the aging Mount Isa lead-zinc underground mine declined, MIM recommended mining in the Black Star open cut, the site of some of MIM's earliest mining operations, aiming to maintain feed to the lead–zinc concentrator. Underground operations in the Mount Isa lead mine then ceased in December 2005, after 75 years of almost continuous operation.

At the time of my arrival back in town in January 2011 there was also a second open-cut operation called "Handlebar Hill" which started production in mid 2008. This operation was mining the high-grade shallow-depth carbonate silver-lead-zinc ore from the Hilton South deposit. The mined ore was trucked along an adjoining haul road and processed in town along with the Black Star ore.

In 2010, Xstrata Zinc announced plans to expand its operations at the Black Star mine to extend its life of mine. The drilling program that would be conducted for the feasibility study into this expansion, is what I was now employed to coordinate.

The Black Star Open Cut Deeps Project already had office space at the Black Star mine and the project manager, Max Shawcross, was getting his team of geologists and engineers together to start the feasibility study. There was already one engineer employed, Ray, and soon there would also be Wade and Charles join the team. Before the drilling commenced, another project geologist was employed to be my back-to-back.

The day Peter Smith started work I was sitting in my office and I sensed someone entering the doorway so turned to see if it was Peter. I nearly fell backwards off my chair when I was startled by a giant of a man taking up the entire doorway. Not only was he 6' 8" tall but he also had the build to go with it, and he had a scar that extended from under his chin, right around the left side of his face and across his forehead – the result of a glassing incident in a pub when he was a teenager. I quickly regained my composure and stood up to welcome him and shake his hand – a hand the size of a baseball mitt, which could have crushed my little girly fingers in a heartbeat. I tried to give as firm a handshake as I could so I didn't portray a weak female geo image – and also to prevent him from crushing my hand unexpectedly.

It didn't take too long to work out that Peter was in fact a gentle giant, and the best partner to work with that I could have hoped for. As we both worked a 2-week on, 1-week off roster, it meant we had one week crossover with both of us on site at the same time.

After being briefed on the scope of work for the drilling program, we both realised how challenging this drilling program was going to be. Actually not so much "challenging" as "the stuff of nightmares"!

All the drill sites were in areas of very high mine traffic – and by traffic I mean 200 tonne dump trucks, 24 hours a day. But it wasn't just what was on the surface we had to worry about. With hundreds of kilometres of underground drives, along with associated water pipes and electrical cables, we had to make sure all of the drillholes avoided underground hazards. This also included human beings who were down there working. The last thing they wanted was to have a drill string break through the back of a drive next to where they were working. The paperwork involved in an incident like that would definitely be the stuff of nightmares and to be avoided at all costs.

Needless to say, the permits we had to prepare for all the drillholes was very extensive – and for good reason. Along with the known hazards, there was also a risk of encountering something unexpectedly because some of the mine records were so old it was impossible to know how reliable they were. Even with all the precautions we took and the all the planning of hole paths in computer models I was still always nervous while drilling near known hazards. Downhole surveys were taken every 30 metres and plotted on the hole path to keep track of where the hole was heading at all times. With the drilling rigs operating 24-hours a day I always slept with my phone next to my pillow in case there was an emergency with the night shift boys intersecting something they shouldn't have. The drillholes were designed and monitored in "Minesite" (the MIM geological drill hole design and management software package) and we adjusted the angles and locations of the holes according to underground infrastructure that could have been in the designed drillhole path.

Along with the dangerous drill sites, there were also the uncomfortable conditions everyone had to work under – particularly the drill crews. With most of the drill holes being around the Black Star pit, it was necessary for everyone at the rig to wear respirators to prevent inhalation of lead dust. While these are uncomfortable at the best of times, we had the added inconvenience of having to wear them in 40-degree heat. I don't know how the guys on the rig managed to survive a 12-hour shift wearing them in that heat.

With the heat being so extreme in Mount Isa there was a very strong focus on hydration and heat stress. All the drill crews were breath tested for alcohol at the start of every shift and once a month MIM required everyone to have a hydration test. And then of course, there was the blood lead levels test, which required a blood sample being taken every 3 – 6 months.

As with all lead mines, we were required to change at the minesite and our work clothes were washed on site. No lead-contaminated work clothes were allowed to be taken off the mine lease. All cars that were driven around the roads on the mine had to be washed down before exiting the mine and driving on town roads. Nothing was easy with this job.

On the plus side though, we had a fantastic group of engineers and geologists in the project team with Peter, Max, Wade and Charles always keeping the team spirit up. The Tom Brown drilling crews and supervisors also helped make the job as much fun as it possibly could be, given the circumstances. I always made sure I held the weekly safety meetings off the mine site and at the Tom Brown Drilling accommodation camp so I was always guaranteed of a free feed and beer after it. The industry provides very few perks these days so you have to take them when you can!

My contract in Mount Isa was for nine months with the drilling program expected to be finished by November. It didn't take long to get settled into my new routine and I decided to start training for another marathon, this time in Barcelona in March. I trained every morning before work with either a run down the Barkly Highway or a weight training session in my apartment. I loved starting the day with a workout so by the time I got to the minesite I was ready to hit the ground running. It was great to see that many of the guys working on the drilling rigs were also into weight training and running and would train after they knocked off work after a 12+ hour shift. The industry had certainly had a cultural shift since the old Rockdril days when everyone just sat around and drank beer after work.

During 2011, CrossFit was gaining a lot of popularity within the fitness industry. I completed a Level 1 Trainer course in Brisbane so I could see what it was all about, and then a few months later while in Washington DC to do the Marine Corps Marathon, I decided to extend my visit by a week and attend a CrossFit Endurance Trainer course in Virginia, USA. The course attendees were mostly military personnel wanting to find out how to train for a marathon and I was one of only two people there who had actually run a marathon before. While the CrossFit philosophy is about performing functional movements that are constantly varied at high intensity, it is a core strength and conditioning program designed to elicit as broad an adaptational response as possible. Like all training regimes there are pros and cons for the program, and I took from it what I knew fitted my personal training style and fitness level. There's no right or wrong exercise program, just whatever works for each individual.

****

Not only had the social side of things changed since I last worked in Mount Isa, but also the work practices at MIM had evolved into a strict safety culture that almost choked you with procedures. You may remember me mentioning how we used to test for TMB's (tuff marker beds) while logging core out at Hilton back in the '90's – etching the rock with hydrofluoric acid simply by tying a vinyl apron around our neck and donning vinyl gloves before reaching our hands inside a fume cupboard. Well the procedure had now evolved into a task that required a written and practical exam and then get signed off by not one, but two different "authorised" people. And then to do the job you had to follow a strict procedure with a trained and authorised observer present and wear the personal protective equipment as modeled below by Peter Smith. And bear in mind it may have been a 40-degree day while you were dressed in this garb. Within minutes there would be a stream of sweat pouring down your back and pooling in your underwear. There's also a set of long work pants and long sleeved shirt underneath that white plastic suit.

****

In late September of 2011 I received an email from Ted at AIPC (Australian-International Petroleum Consultants) to say he had a wellsite geology job for me working offshore for ConocoPhillips and the expected start date was in

253

October. With my contract at MIM due to wind up in late October it was perfect timing so I gave four weeks notice at Black Star knowing that the drilling program there would have been completed by then. Peter Smith had also indicated he would be finishing up at the end of contract date so we were both looking at finishing at the same time. But then Max gave us the news that they now wanted to do some further drilling at the old Rio Grande Open Cut site at the southern end of the mine lease which would mean another few months work beyond October.

In a twist of fate, Ted advised me that the start date for the ConocoPhillips job had been pushed back by a few months while they were waiting on a rig to become available which meant I could then stay on and continue with the MIM drilling program. With Peter already committed to leaving it meant I would be the only geologist for the next few months so I worked for a couple of weeks at a time and took a few days off, with my French fieldy Flo taking charge of the rigs in my absence. By this stage we had employed a contract geologist, Sarah, to help us with the core logging so Flo and I managed the drilling program between the two of us. The lengthy permitting process and difficult drill site preparation was very time-consuming so we were kept busy making sure the rigs had a site to go to after completing each hole.

By the end of March 2012, the drilling was all but completed and I finally got word that the ConocoPhillips job was starting in early April. It was time for me to pack up my car and start the long drive back to the Gold Coast.

Chapter 20

2012 - 2014

CONOCOPHILLIPS
BROWSE BASIN, WA

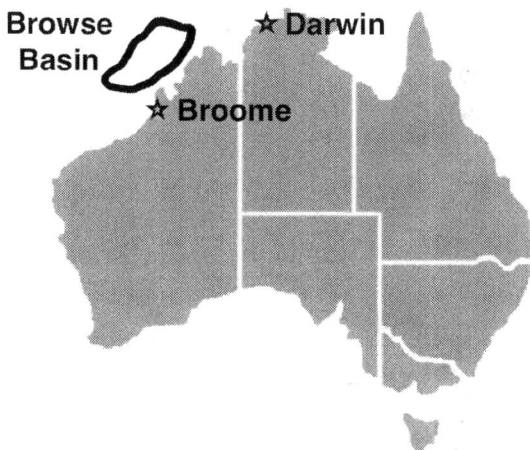

Once the paperwork was completed for the ConocoPhillips contract, I had a company medical done on the Gold Coast before flying over to Perth for a briefing then heading to the rig. After a day in the ConocoPhillips office, meeting the operations team, and then an afternoon in the AIPC office, having a crash refresher course in using R-WEB, it was time to fly to the Transocean Legend in the Browse Basin and get started.

The Browse Basin is an offshore basin on the northwestern Australian margin. The basin is a proven hydrocarbon province, with major undeveloped gas/condensate fields in the outer and central basin and minor oil discoveries on the basin's eastern margin. The basin is set to become a new, significant source of global LNG supply by 2020.

With ConocoPhillips being the operator, and holding a 60% interest in Exploration Permits WA-315-P and WA-398-P, and 10% interest in WA-314-P, they were exploring for natural gas and condensate in the Greater Poseidon field within the Browse Basin, approximately 480 km north of Broome.

Phase one of exploration commenced in 2009, with a four well drilling program. The first well, Poseidon-1, was a successful discovery. Drilling continued into 2010 with two wells, Poseidon-2 and Kronos-1, successfully encountering hydrocarbons. I was about to start working on their second phase of exploration drilling for which six wells were planned, with the principal objective of the exploration program being to better define the size and quality of the hydrocarbon accumulations within the exploration permits which contain the greater Poseidon trend. The wells were expected to take about 18 months to complete and I was very excited to be getting the chance to start working on a long-term drilling campaign and being part of the team on the Transocean Legend.

The Transocean Legend was a semi-submersible rig with bed space for 128 people. It was an old rig that still had a communal bathroom for the people who were unfortunate enough to have to share 4-man rooms with no ensuite bathroom. Fortunately I was in one of the better rooms and only had to share it with the other wellsite geologist who was on board, which meant we had the room to ourselves while off-shift. Although it's not a written rule, it's generally accepted that when you share a room with somebody you don't go back into the room until your back-to-back starts their shift and leaves the room. This rule became even more relevant when you were sharing with the opposite sex – and they were married! I actually preferred sharing with a male worker as I had the rare occasion where I was put in a room with other females and the bedroom and bathroom would be full of girly crap. Knowing how much it annoyed me, I was always conscious of never leaving any of my gear lying around in the bedroom or bathroom, instead storing it all in the locker provided for each person in the room.

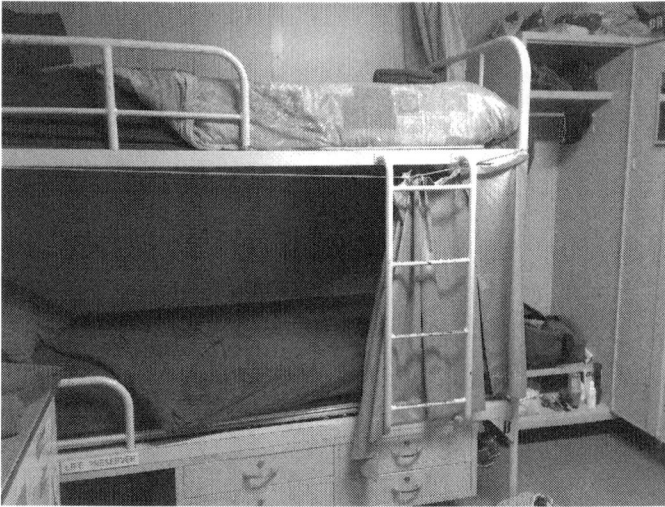

The hitches were 4-weeks on, 4-weeks off and I had to fly from Brisbane to Perth, then on to Broome where the helicopter departed from. With the rig being so far offshore, it was necessary to make a stop at the Lombadina airstrip to top up the fuel on the way out to the rig. Lombadina is a small community on the Dampier Peninsula, approximately 185km by road from Broome. The trip to the rig would take about two and a half hours from the time we left Broome airport.

The Browse Basin lies in the body of water bordering the Indian Ocean and the Timor Sea and has a tropical climate. The coastline of this part of Australia is famous for its unusually large tidal ranges and has been recorded as having the second largest tide ranges in the world. The intertidal zone (the area between low and high tides) can be tens of kilometres wide — compared to just a few metres on the east coast of Australia. People have been known to get caught out on local beaches at low tide and having the tide come in so fast, they have to make a run for it to beat the water back to shore.

The tides here are commonly referred to as "macro" tides, rather than king tides. Macro tides are much larger than the normal high tides caused by the action of the moon, because they are also influenced by the shape of the local coast. The coastline north of Broome is an extension of the wide, shallow northwest continental shelf. When the water comes in from deeper areas, it is constricted and squeezed by the shallow continental shelf. Because the volume of water is being constrained in this shallow region, the currents increase to try and move the water onto the shelf, with the tide being amplified as it moves shoreward.

ConocoPhillips previous drilling program in 2009-2010 intersected gas-bearing sandstone packages in the Plover Formation, and also a gas zone in the overlying Montara Formation. With a known pressure ramp in the Jamieson Formation the wells were drilled under strict HPHT (High Pressure High Temperature) conditions with flow-back fingerprinting being undertaken and monitored diligently throughout the drilling of all the wells. The second well that was drilled included a cored section through the gas-bearing sandstones, to undertake reservoir characterisation studies.

Throughout the drilling program we maintained a core team of three wellsite geologists, with me, Mike Kenny and

Jimmy Concepcion cross-shifting with each other for the entire campaign, and quite a succession of other highly-experienced wellsite geologists filling in as the fourth geologist.

The "Legend" was part of the Transocean fleet of rigs that also had included the ill-fated Deepwater Horizon semi-submersible rig. On 20 April 2010, while drilling at the Macondo Prospect in the Gulf of Mexico, an explosion on the Deepwater Horizon caused by a blowout killed 11 crewmen and ignited a fireball visible from 64 km (40 mi) away. The resulting fire could not be extinguished and, on 22 April 2010, Deepwater Horizon sank.

My first hitch on the "Legend" coincided with the 2nd anniversary of the Deepwater Horizon tragedy and it was commemorated with a memorial service held on the helideck to remember all those who perished in the disaster. It was a sombre reminder of the dangers that face us while working offshore. As we were congregated on the helideck, suspended high over the water and with only the turquoise waters of the Indian Ocean visible for as far as the eye could see, it was a timely reminder of how vulnerable and exposed we were to unexpected events that can occur during drilling. We can only hope that lessons learnt from such disasters help us to avoid future ones.

Having a permanent 4-week rotation meant I could plan holidays and I took advantage of it by running more marathons around the world. In November of 2012, I ran the Antarctic Ice Marathon, on the Union Glacier in Antarctica, which saw me become a member of the Seven Continents Marathon Club, after previously running a marathon on all the other six continents around the world.

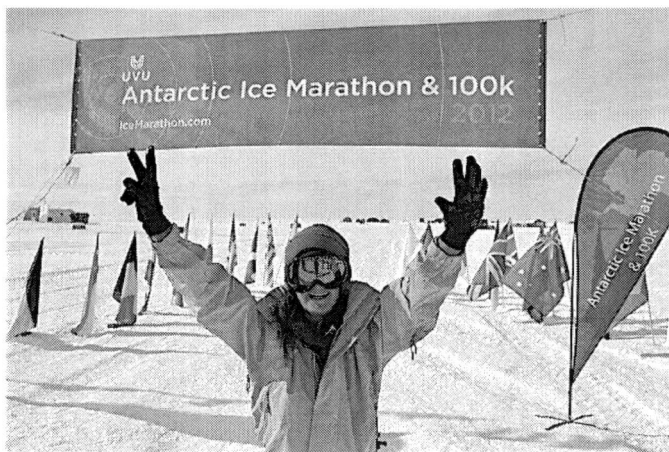

The London marathon and Gold Coast marathons in 2009 gave me Europe and Australasia, and in October of 2011 I completed the Marine Corps Marathon in Washington DC, which gave me a North American marathon. In 2012 I set myself a goal of completing a marathon on all the remaining continents and succeeded by running the Kilimanjaro Marathon in Tanzania, the Great Wall Marathon in China, the Inca Trail Marathon in Peru, and finally the Antarctic Ice Marathon in November.

The Inca Trail Marathon was the toughest, yet most amazing, marathon I have done and saw me running the marathon in 8 hours and 50 minutes along the Inca Trail, which normally takes tourists three days to complete. The sight of 26 runners in shorts and singlet tops running past the back-packing hikers had all the tourists scratching their heads, but they enthusiastically cheered us on as the runners passed by.

During 2012 I also achieved a goal of obtaining a Boston Marathon qualifying time at the Perth Marathon in June 2012. To "qualify" for the Boston Marathon (or "BQ") runners need to have run a marathon at a time given for their gender and age. My "BQ" time for 50-55 year-old women was 4:00 hours and I managed to finish the Perth Marathon in 3:56:59, which automatically qualified me for a registration in the 2013 Boston Marathon.

Begun in 1897, inspired by the success of the first modern-day marathon competition in the 1896 Summer Olympics, the Boston Marathon is the world's oldest annual marathon and ranks as one of the world's best-known road racing events. (*2016 was the 120th running of the Boston Marathon*). Though starting with only 18 participants in 1897, the event now attracts an average of over 30,000 registered participants each year.

While I was able to run my qualifying race in under 4 hours, I went a bit slower in the actual Boston Marathon, taking photos and lapping up the crowd atmosphere along the route from Hopkinton to Boylston Street in Boston. When only 1 km from the finish line I encountered a wall of runners who had, for some unknown reason, come to a standstill along the race route, crammed within the barricades along the road blocking the cheering spectators from the race participants. I was only minutes from crossing the finish line at the famous Boston Marathon and I could no longer continue – I couldn't even imagine at the time what would have made the entire race stop. When I turned and saw a young guy sitting on the road behind me on his mobile phone I asked if he knew why we were stopped, and he replied that apparently bombs were let off at the finish line. Knowing that if that were true, it would have been shown on TV worldwide, I sent a text message to my family saying I was OK and then rang my son on the Gold Coast. He was in bed asleep as it was only 5 am local time, but I asked him to get up and turn on the TV and see if it was on the news, so I could confirm if it was correct, as there was no news filtering down to the runners stranded on the course at this stage. A few minutes later I received a text message back from my son saying: "bombs gone off...don't know how many dead yet...don't go near the finish line...get the f*** out of there!" And the rest is history, as they say. My first attempt at the Boston Marathon ended just six city blocks short of the finish line. In 2014 I went back and did it all again – and this time I got to run down Boylston Street and across the finish line!

As well as running four marathons in Australia through 2013 (one of which I ran my personal best time of 3 hrs 47 min to get a qualifying time for the New York City Marathon in 2014), I also competed in the "Jungle Marathon", which is an unsupported, multi-stage, ultra-endurance race through the Amazon Jungle in Brazil. That race was worthy of a book all of its own and you can read about it in my first published book called "Call Of The Jungle – How a Camping-Hating City-Slicker Mum Survived an Ultra Endurance Race through the Amazon Jungle" (*Available in print and kindle version on Amazon.com*).

My race calendar for 2013 finished with the Honolulu Marathon in Hawaii on my birthday in December – what better way to see the New Year in than running 42.2 km around the Waikiki headlands!

In July of 2013 I was surprised to find out my running exploits had somehow reached an advertising agency in Amsterdam and I received the following message from them:

"I am writing to you from 180 Amsterdam. We are an international creative agency who creates ideas and advertising campaigns for global brands. We are currently working in partnership with Asics on their 2014 campaign, which revolves around the concept of self-belief, continual improvement, and striving to be more. As part of this project, we will be creating a series of inspiring short films that together chart a journey of athletic improvement from beginning to end. Each film will feature a different everyday or professional athlete at a particular stage in their journey, and will deliver an inspiring personal insight into what it takes to be the best that you can be.

We would very much like to dedicate one of these short films towards a marathon runner who is forced to train in unusual circumstances such as on an oil rig or a ship at sea. We want to tell the inspiring story of how dedicated they are, not only to running 26.2 miles, but overcoming everyday challenges even in the training process, highlighting their dedication while inspiring others around them.

We read about your unique story and were fascinated. We knew that others would want to hear your story as well. Running a marathon is a feat in its own, one that only 1% of the population will ever challenge themselves to. But what we don't hear about are the extreme challenges in environment that one has to overcome just to get to the starting line. We were wondering if you would be interested in a phone call with us to hear more about your challenges training on the offshore rig and also for the Antarctica marathon."

After a few emails back and forth they said they wanted to send a film crew down to Australia and film me training on the rig. At that point I realised there was probably next-to-no chance of getting permission for a film crew to come onto the rig so I checked with the Transocean OIM (Offshore Installation Manager) Lawrence, and he was happy for me to do it but then ConocoPhillips knocked it on the head – as I suspected. So my three minutes of fame disappeared as quickly as it came.

****

I worked night shift for the entire drilling campaign while I was on the Legend, starting at 6 pm and finishing at 6 am, every day for 28 days straight throughout each hitch. I didn't care what shift I worked on as we worked in offices with no windows and slept in a bedroom with no windows, so you never saw daylight anyway except when walking from the mudlogging unit to the accommodation for meals.

It was always a bit of a shock to my eyes when we had day-time fire drills on a Sunday and I'd have to go up onto the helideck in the bright sunlight after being woken up in the dark room by the fire alarm. I had to make sure I took my sunglasses up with me so I wasn't blinded by that big, bright yellow thing in the sky.

By the end of the Browse Basin drilling campaign the crew on the Legend had become quite a close-knit team. With Kurt, the night company man, on the job there was always the smell of hot popcorn drifting around the offices during the night – sometimes it got a bit too close to "smoking hot popcorn that threatened to set off the fire alarms and sprinklers in the entire accommodation block" kind-of-smell, but Kurt always had it under control.

I was surprised to learn that men can even annoy their wives without ever having to be home, by changing the channel on the TV at home while their wife is watching her favourite program. Foxtel's mobile app now means no one is spared of a channel-surfing husband – even if they're on an oilrig in the Indian Ocean. I was equally impressed at the cursory text message that the logistics co-ordinator Darren, received from his wife in response to his interruption to her TV program at home in Melbourne. I can't even imagine how annoying he must be when he's actually at home!

And how could I forget the pre-tour meeting on Christmas day in 2013. Everyone knows the rig isn't your first choice of where you'd like to be on Christmas day so the company man at the time decided to give a speech to remind the workers of their unfortunate roster timing. It went something like: "We're all stuck out here so we don't give a f*** what you think - just f*** the hell up and do your job". I was actually feeling OK about having to work over Christmas until that rant, (trust me, it went on and on and on!) as was everyone else in the room, but somehow any Christmas cheer we had was just turned into dumbfounded disbelief. Talk about a Christmas Grinch.

****

As the last well of the campaign was winding up it was time to start looking for another job. The rig was heading up to the Timor Sea to do a couple of development wells for ConocoPhillips but it would be a few months before they would be drilling again and the wellsite geology positions had to be advertised so there was no guarantee I would still be kept on. I didn't want to wait for 3 months, with no pay, for the job to start and then find out I didn't get it anyway. I couldn't risk that happening so started to see what else was available straight away.

I sent AIPC an email to see if they had any other jobs on their books, and also emailed Peter Gibson of Reservoir Dogs (*the very same Peter Gibson who was the first wellsite geologist I ever worked with offshore and taught me how to describe samples*), who had emailed me earlier in the year to see if I was interested in some work he was tendering for. Reservoir Dogs, like AIPC, is an agency that provides consultant wellsite geologists and operations geologists to the oil and gas industry.

I got an almost immediate reply from Peter to say that he just had a position come up with Woodside Energy Ltd so would submit my resume to the company and see if they were prepared to employ me. Within a few days I got the word that I was accepted and would be starting as soon as I could get the company medical and paperwork done.

After nearly two years on the Transocean Legend it was time to leave. The one set of accommodation clothes and gym clothes that I wore every day for two years got thrown in the bin and I packed my work boots into a bag and caught a chopper off the rig for the last time. The Transocean Legend has since been cut up for scrap metal but the legend of the Legend lives on!

Chapter 21

2014 - 2015

WOODSIDE, OFFSHORE WA

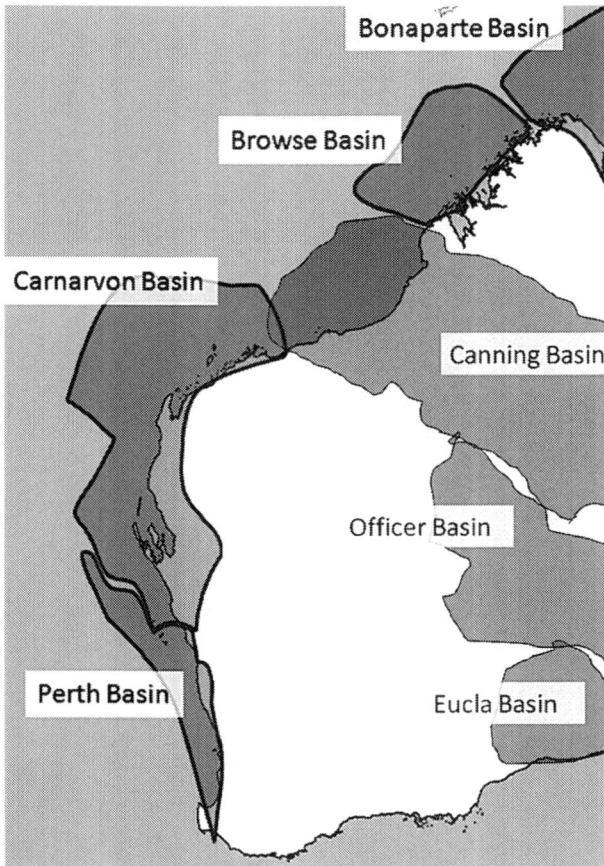

Bonaparte Basin

Browse Basin

Carnarvon Basin

Canning Basin

Officer Basin

Perth Basin

Eucla Basin

Woodside Petroleum Limited is an Australian petroleum exploration and production company and is the largest operator of oil and gas production in Australia. It's also Australia's largest independent dedicated oil and gas company.

Woodside was incorporated on 26 July 1954. It was originally named Woodside (Lakes Entrance) Oil Co NL and it was named after the small town of Woodside, Victoria. Woodside's early years were focused on Victoria's Gippsland Basin. Switching to northern Western Australia in the early 1960s, Woodside joined up with Shell and Burmah Oil to form the original North West Shelf consortium. They now hold the following producing assets on the North West Shelf: Karratha Gas plant, Goodwyn A platform, North Rankin Complex, Okha FPSO (floating, production, storage and offloading vessel), Angel platform, Pluto LNG plant, Pluto LNG platform, Ngujima-Yin FPSO and the Nganhurra FPSO.

Woodside's exploration portfolio includes emerging and frontier provinces in Australia and the Asia-Pacific region, the Atlantic margins and Latin America and Sub-Saharan Africa.

Woodside had already drilled one well of the current drilling campaign and were just starting on the second when I arrived on the Deepwater Millennium drillship. The exploration wells were to be drilled in the Outer Canning Basin, Outer Carnarvon Basin and Northern Carnarvon Basin of the North West Shelf of Western Australia, and would also include some coring operations. Water depths would be up to nearly 1,000 metres (3,280 feet) on some locations so a drillship with dynamic positioning capabilities was required.

Transocean's Deepwater Millennium (DWM) is a fifth generation dynamic positioned (DP) drillship. It is capable of drilling in water depths up to approximately 3,000 metres (10,000 feet) and drilling to depths of about 9,000 metres (30,000 feet).

Rather than being anchored to the seabed, like shallow-water jack-up rigs and semi-submersible rigs, the Millennium uses dynamic positioning whereby a computer-controlled system automatically maintains the vessel's position and heading by using its own propellers and thrusters. Position reference sensors, combined with wind sensors, motion sensors and gyrocompasses, provide information to the computer pertaining to the vessel's position and the magnitude and direction of environmental forces affecting its position.

Dynamic positioned ships have three possible levels of classification, with the Millennium having the highest system of Equipment Class 3. DPS-3 classification refers to a system, which has a redundancy system so that no single fault in an active system can cause the system to fail. It can withstand a fire or flood in any one compartment without the system failing, which is achieved by having two independent computer systems with a separate back-up system. There are two dynamic positioning officers on shift at all times to make sure the system is working effectively. The consequences of the ship drifting off well centre while the drill pipe is connecting the ship to the seabed can be catastrophic and vigilance in maintaining integrity of the dynamic positioning system is paramount.

Unlike the rest of the workplaces on the rig, the bridge is a spacious, quiet, clean office with the best views in the "building". It looks more like the flight deck on the "Starship Enterprise" than a bridge on a drilling rig. Everyone appears to talk in hushed tones and keeps to themselves – well that's what it seems like after working out on the deck where everyone is screaming at each other to be heard over the noise of the rig.

If there was ever an emergency situation on the rig, all operations are performed from this room. The "radio operator" also works out of the bridge and is in direct communication with shore-based operations and emergency services at all times. Weekly fire and abandon-rig drills are performed from this office and emergency drillfloor shut-in procedures can be operated from independent systems at the bridge in the event of an uncontrolled "blow-out" while drilling.

The Deepwater Millennium is a Transocean rig and

several crew members from the Transocean Legend had been transferred onto this rig, so there were a few familiar faces when I arrived on the decks.

Being a drillship meant there are a lot more people required for operations as there needs to be a full marine crew, as well as the drill crew. The DWM had bed space for 180 people and was therefore a much bigger rig than I'd been on before. Although the rig had been in service since 1999, it had undergone an upgrade in 2013 and had new accommodation blocks added to it. Accommodation levels went from A-deck to E-deck, with the galley/mess room on A-deck and my cabin on E-deck. While there was a lift in the accommodation block it was usually faster just to take the stairs.

Being a big rig meant there was also a big, spacious gym. The gym was on a lower deck below A-deck and down in the bowels of the rig. Sadly it had no windows but it more than made up for it with its size. There was a separate room with cardio equipment and not just one, but two treadmills, along with other equipment. Then there was the main weights room that included a Smith Machine and full set of dumb bells up to about 50kg amongst all the other equipment, plus another small room off that which had a squat rack. And for the hard core trainers there was a room off the cardio room that led out into the un-air-conditioned storage space of the rig which had a boxing bag, chin-up bar and dips rack – how could you want for anything else?!

Like all the other rigs I had worked on, the DWM had a remotely operated vehicle (ROV), which monitored the

273

subsea operations. The ROV has cameras that relay images of what can be seen on the seabed and along the length of the marine riser pipe, which connects the ship to the seabed, via the Lower Marine Riser Package (LMRP) and the Blow Out Preventer (BOP).

The wells that were drilled in shallower water usually had quite a bit of marine life visible from the ROV cameras and the operators made an effort to capture footage of any unusual sea creatures they came across. With very little of the earth's subsea life routinely captured on film, the information the ROV's on offshore facilities can provide is an invaluable source of data for marine researchers. At the deeper water depths there were some really weird jellyfish spotted and even a species that was thought to be previously unknown.

The Millennium had an extensive closed circuit TV monitoring system with cameras in all the key areas of the rig. The mudlogging unit had a TV screen so we could monitor operations while working inside the unit. We were able to view operations on the drillfloor, shaker house, pit room, helideck and many other areas, as well as seeing the view from the ROV cameras.

****

When you're one of only a few women on a rig with over one hundred men there's always a chance that one day you could literally get caught with your pants down. The doors on the bedrooms are supposed to remain unlocked at all times so that in the event of an emergency the rooms can be checked.

Up until now, I'd managed to escape being caught

unexpectedly in my room…but my luck was about to change. Flying onto the rig at the start of one of the wells, I was the first wellsite geologist on board and needed to call casing point for the top section of the hole. As there are no cuttings to the surface for the drilling of this section, they don't need two geologists, which meant I was on-call 24 hours a day. It's impossible to predict an exact time they will drill into the zone of interest, and after being in the mudlogging unit for over 12 hours already I decided to go to bed, but gave the mudloggers instructions to send someone to wake me up if they got to a certain depth during the night.

During the middle of the night there was a knock on my cabin door, which woke me, and then the data engineer partially opened the door and poked his head through to tell me they were at the depth I'd requested to be woken. I thanked him and said I'd head over to the logging unit straight away. After he shut the door I climbed down from the bunk bed and went to the bathroom to have a quick shower before heading back to work.

At the exact moment I opened the bathroom door after my shower to walk back into the room, the data engineer poked his head back through my cabin door, which was less than a metre from where I was standing – totally naked. I froze on the spot, not sure whether to laugh or scream, while he continued to stand there and explain that he was just checking that I hadn't fallen back to sleep because it had been a while since he first woke me and I hadn't come out of the room. I think he did knock before entering but I must have been in the shower and didn't hear it so when he had no response he thought he'd better check. To his credit, he didn't laugh or scream in horror and when I arrived back in the logging unit he was totally professional and acted as if nothing had happened.

During the next hitch on the Millennium, a cyclone was forming north of where we were drilling and its status was being monitored closely. As it can take a few days to secure the rig if a cyclone was to hit, it's necessary to start evacuating people well ahead of time. Normally the ship would just sail out of the danger zone and all personnel would stay on the vessel and return to the well location when it's safe to do so, but as they were at a point in the drilling operations where they wouldn't be needing a geologist on board for a while, then we were likely to get evacuated off the rig if they decided to take precautionary action.

When I knocked off at the end of my shift I knew there was a chance we may have been evacuated off the rig the next morning but the decision still hadn't been made before I headed to my room so I carried on as normal until I heard otherwise. I was just stepping out of the bathroom after a shower when the other wellsite geologist stuck his head through the door of our cabin – just as I was standing next to the door totally naked – again!

He had come to let me know that we would be on the chopper the next morning as they started evacuating people off the rig, so thought he'd better inform me before going to bed so I could pack my bags as soon as I got up in the morning. He apparently knocked on the door before entering but again; I must have been in the shower at the time and didn't hear the knock. Unfortunately for him, he was visibly traumatised from the encounter and all he could say at the time was: "Oh my God, my worst fear!" I was able to see the funny side of it but I don't think he did.

While working offshore Western Australia, we would normally work a 3-week hitch but this was very unpredictable, as our hitches were dependent on drilling operations. If they were drilling we would stay on the rig, if they weren't drilling we would leave. We could be on the rig anywhere from only a few days to four weeks, which is the maximum allowed for health and safety reasons. Although there was a rough roster we were following, this always changed from day-to-day because of the drilling. At one stage I had to change my return flights home four times before I finally got to leave the rig. Unexpected drilling delays can hit at any time and we have to be prepared to stay on the rig for as long as it takes to complete the drilling and wireline operations.

****

During one of my breaks from the rig, I travelled to Houston, Texas, to complete a weeklong Petroskills course on Wireline Formation Testing and Interpretation. I was fortunate enough to be passing through Los Angeles on my way home on the same weekend the LA Marathon was being run. I managed to "kill two birds with the one stone" and got an overseas marathon done while pursuing further study…bonus!

****

As the Carnarvon and Canning Basin drilling campaign came to an end, Woodside continued with the Deepwater Millennium contract to conduct three wells offshore from Korea and Myanmar, with the wellsite geologists continuing on with it.

Working out of South Korea meant having another company medical, as well as travel vaccinations for Japanese Encephalitis, typhoid, diphtheria and tetanus booster, rabies and influenza. Hepatitis A and B and yellow fever vaccinations were also required but I was already covered for those from previous travel I had done overseas. My shoulders were feeling very sore and sorry after leaving the travel doctors office.

As well as the travel vaccinations, I also had to re-do my sea survival and HUET (Helicopter Underwater Escape Training) as I was only accredited for tropical water since doing my refresher only 12 months before. Because the weather can be freezing in South Korea in the winter months, there was a chance we'd have to wear survival suits on the choppers so a cold water HUET was required.

With the medicals and vaccinations all completed, it was time to fly to the South Korean port city of Busan where the helicopters would leave from to fly to the Deepwater Millennium.

Chapter 22

2015

WOODSIDE, ULLEUNG BASIN, SOUTH KOREA

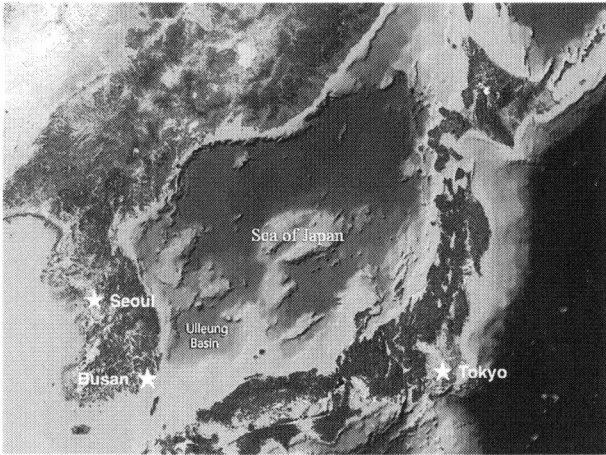

Busan (known locally as Pusan) is South Korea's second largest city after Seoul, with a population of approximately 3.6 million. The city is located on the southeastern-most tip of the Korean peninsula. It is the largest port city in South Korea and the world's fifth busiest seaport by cargo tonnage.

The most densely built up areas of the city are situated in a number of narrow valleys between the Nakdong and Suyeong Rivers, with mountains separating most of the districts. The helicopter ride out to the rig gave us fantastic views of the densely populated city as we flew at low altitude along the river and out to sea. It was hard to ignore the military presence in the area, with three navy ships forming a small armada along the coastline, heading north into the Sea of Japan as we flew overhead.

****

The Ulleung Basin is located in the East Sea, between Korea and Japan. Woodside and its partner, Korean National Oil Corporation (KNOC), agreed to explore deepwater blocks, Block 6-1 North and Block 8, and in 2012 the exploration well Jujak-1 was drilled to test the extension of the petroleum system that was proven by the producing fields on the shelf to the south (operated by KNOC). This was followed by a 3D seismic survey of the area in 2014 which helped define the target for this second exploration well, Hongge-1, which the Deepwater Millennium was about to drill.

The crew on the Millennium now consisted of a lot more Korean nationals than Australians, with only the more senior Transocean personnel travelling with the rig after departing Australian waters. Many of the third party companies on the rig were also now sourcing staff from their Asian bases rather than Australia, so there was now an even greater mix of nationalities working on the rig than previously.

The catering crew and cleaners were all from either Korea or other Asian centres and they were 100% male so there were even fewer females on the rig now. With such a high percentage of National workers who spoke very little English, it was necessary to have a translator working on the rig who could repeat all important PA and meeting announcements in Korean. There were also KNOC geologists and drilling engineers on the rig to observe the drilling operations. It was great having the local knowledge on board and the Korean guests were not only a valuable source of information on the Ulleung Basin but also on tourist things to do while we had a stop-over in Busan on our way home. I was surprised to learn from KNOC Geologist Ingyong, that Busan is home to the world's largest department store after the Shinsegae flagship store in Centum City, Busan, claimed the long held record from Macy's, in New York City, in 2009.

From the well location we could just make out the eastern coastline of South Korea, although most of the time the smog was too severe to be able to see it. At night you could see the orange glow, encapsulated in the smog, from the lights of the large cities dotted along the coastline. There were also bright lights from the many squid fishing vessels in the area. There seemed to be no fish in the waters here, which was strange after working on the North West Shelf with its abundant marine life. I'm guessing the sea here was all fished out by the millions of people who live around its shores. Judging by the number of squid fishing vessels out on the waters during the night there must still be lots of squid swimming around out there.

With the sea being virtually land-locked by the Korean peninsular to the west and Japan to the east, the water was always very calm. The rig was so stable most of the time you wouldn't have even known we were floating. Being such a huge vessel meant it was normally quite stable even in moderately rough conditions but given the calm water we were on out there I was always guaranteed of a flat run on the treadmill.

The body of water we were drilling in was a very busy marine channel for not only merchant vessels but also military vessels. But it wasn't only the sea that had a military presence. While we were unloading wireline tools on the deck one afternoon we could hear a strange, distant whistling noise above all the rig noise, and were surprised to see two fighter jets circling high above the rig. We stood and watched in excited amazement until we realised they were coming lower and lower, spiraling down towards us in tight formation. Our excitement soon turned to panic as we considered the possibility of them not being friendly fighter jets at all, and maybe we were now a target in their crosshairs as they defended their territory. Just as I was thinking "have I got time to run up the six flights of stairs to the wireline unit to send my kids an email to say I love them?" the jets roared out of their downward spiral and leveled off, travelling south and away from the rig. Phew, that was a relief! Our nervous expressions turned to laughter as we watched the jets disappear in the distance and out of harms way.

****

The water depth where we were drilling was 1,952 metres (6,404 feet), which was the deepest water I had ever drilled in. There was no interesting marine life visible on the seabed through the ROV cameras, just darkness.

The extensive distance from the drillfloor to the seabed meant that the drilling fluid experienced a considerable cooling effect while travelling into, and out of the well. The main functions of drilling fluids include providing hydrostatic pressure to prevent formation fluids from entering into the well bore, and to avoid formation damage. The properties of the "mud" can vary with temperature so these properties had to be very carefully monitored throughout the drilling to ensure the integrity of the mud system.

Despite being on the other side of the world from Woodside's Perth office, everyone there was able to view the well information in real time as it was being drilled. Drilling parameters, LWD (Logging While Drilling) and mud gas values were transmitted continuously not only within the mudlogging unit on the rig, but also via a satellite communications link to Perth so the onshore operations teams could keep up-to-date with what was happening. The dissemination of information to all parties involved in the drilling was a 24-hour process and the wellsite geologists are the conduits by which geological and drilling data is relayed to, and from the rig. This was never more important when we were expecting to drill into the prognosed reservoir section. The petrophysicists and drilling engineers in Perth closely monitored the progress as we drilled through the claystone seal and penetrated the expected reservoir sandstone, with everyone remaining vigilant for any indications of unexpected changes in drilling parameters. Well control issues are more likely to occur in the reservoir section than in any other section of the well so everyone, offshore and onshore, is on high alert during this phase of the drilling. Wireline logging will later be run based on what is encountered during the drilling of the reservoir section. Any geological information that couldn't be obtained during the drilling of the well will be obtained during wireline operations, including the collection of reservoir fluid samples and formation core samples.

While the Hongge-1 exploration well confirmed the presence of a petroleum system with a significant gas column within the primary target, a high percentage of inert gas in the hydrocarbon column resulted in it being declared a non-commercial discovery. The information gained from this well would now be used to evaluate any other possible targets within the deepwater block.

****

Within 48 hours of the last wireline run being performed, myself and the other wellsite geologist Mitch Tomlinson were sent off the rig. With plug and abandon operations now underway, a geologist is no longer needed on the rig.

The helicopter arrived back in Busan too late for me to make a connecting flight to Singapore so I had to stay overnight in the hotel that Woodside were using as their crew transit stopover in Busan. The reception area of this hotel had a room set aside where the Woodside ground logistics team processed all the incoming and outgoing Deepwater Millennium personnel. With a large hand gun sitting visibly on the desk amongst the paperwork, I wasn't sure how safe this city was but I decided to go for a walk to get something for lunch anyway.

I was advised by the hotel staff to catch the nearby train to the next station where there were plenty of options for dining. I first had to go to the bank to exchange some money and as I entered the building I was surprised to be greeted by an elderly bank employee who turned to reveal a pistol stuffed down the waistband of his suit pants. I guess no one takes their safety for granted in Busan.

After spending a comfortable night in a hotel room that was obviously decorated to suit travelling businessmen, I left Busan for the trip back to Brisbane, via Seoul and Singapore. On discovering that the Seoul Marathon was to be run just a few days after I was travelling through the city, I was tempted to stay and participate in it but I was already booked to do the Havana Marathon, in Cuba just two weeks later during my break so I decided against it. The desire to get home and sleep in my own bed won out over staying in Seoul and running a marathon.

My next hitch on the Millennium was to be offshore from Myanmar so I knew there would be a longer than usual break while the rig completed the plug and abandon operations on Hongge-1 and then sailed around to Myanmar and set up for the next well. As usual, I wouldn't know exactly when I'd be needed again until probably a few days before I needed to leave home so I had to keep my diary free so I was prepared to leave at short notice around the time I was expecting the rig to be on the next location.

Chapter 23

2015 - 2016

WOODSIDE, RAKHINE BASIN, MYANMAR

Myanmar, formally known as Burma, is one of the poorest nations in Southeast Asia, suffering from decades of stagnation, mismanagement and isolation but it's also one of the oldest oil producing countries in the world with onshore oil production dating back to the thirteenth century. Although a large number of oilfields have been discovered most are small, however significant oil and gas potential still remains as Myanmar is considered under-explored by industry standards.

The Rakhine Basin is one of six major geological provinces in Myanmar with the onshore basins being prospective for oil and the offshore areas considered to be strongly gas-prone. A major portion of the basin is offshore and the few shallow water offshore wells already drilled in the basin only extended to the Lower Pliocene and the understanding of deeper stratigraphy is mostly from onshore wells.

The onshore/offshore Cretaceous to Pliocene Rakhine Basin is located along the west coast of Myanmar, and extends into the Bay of Bengal. It is bounded to the east by the Indo-Burman Ranges and to the west by the ocean trench marking the northern extension of the Andaman Subduction Zone. The basin extends north into Bangladesh and in the south it narrows and merges with the Andaman fore-arc basin.

Myanmar Oil and Gas Enterprise (MOGE) conducted three international bidding rounds for a number of onshore and offshore blocks after the nominally civilian government took office in 2011. Before this, as a result of Western sanctions, a majority of investors into Myanmar's oil and gas sector were Asian companies.

The first onshore bidding round for 18 blocks was launched in 2011 and 9 blocks were awarded to international companies. In 2013, the second onshore bidding round for 18 blocks and the first offshore round for 30 blocks were launched. Of these, a total of 16 onshore and 20 offshore blocks were awarded. Myanmar has a total of 104 oil and gas blocks including 53 onshore and 51 offshore blocks with 16 onshore and 19 offshore blocks currently in operation.

During the 2013 Myanmar Offshore Bid Round, Woodside secured interests in six different permits covering a combined area of 46,000 km2, making the Australian energy company the largest acreage holder in the emerging Rakhine Basin. After undertaking social and environmental impact assessment surveys and seismic acquisition activities, Woodside was now preparing to drill the first of two deepwater exploration wells in the Rakhine Basin.

Exploration well Shwe Yee Htun-1 was to be drilled approximately 60 km offshore in water depth of nearly 2,000 metres. The Deepwater Millennium drillship was already on location and preparing to spud the well when I arrived in Yangon on the 17th December. This would be my fourth year in a row of spending Christmas and New Year working offshore on a rig, but I was happy to volunteer for it so the geologists who had young children could spend it at home.

Upon exiting the customs at Yangon International Airport, I was met by a Woodside company representative who was holding up an iPad with my name displayed on it. He was a Yangon local but spoke very good English and as he led me out to the driveway pick-up area outside the terminal building he handed me a vinyl pouch and instructed me to unzip it and retrieve the contents from inside. It contained a cardboard folder with documents explaining the Woodside ground logistics details and emergency contact numbers for people and places of importance should I need assistance during my transit through Yangon. There was also a mobile phone in the pouch that I could use to contact the Woodside office in Yangon or for any other use while I was in town. My

Australian mobile phone was unable to pick up a local carrier, despite having a Telstra account back home and being activated for international roaming.

I was required to read all the documents and sign off to say I'd read them all and understood the requirements. I was starting to feel like a spy being briefed on my secret mission – should I choose to accept it!

After about 10 minutes, a car pulled up and I was introduced to the driver of the private security firm's car who was contracted to help Woodside employees get around town. I would be driven to the Woodside office first to meet the local team, and then taken to my hotel where I would overnight before heading out to the rig early the next morning.

Once I had settled into the back seat of the car I pulled out the mobile phone from the pouch and was surprised at the ancient Nokia model phone. This was no smart phone – more like an original Nokia that first hit the market all those years ago. I couldn't even remember how to use one of these so I was hoping I wouldn't have an emergency and need to use it.

After twenty hours of flights and airport stopovers it was a welcoming relief to finally be only a short drive away from checking into a hotel room, but the chaotic densely populated city was going to make the short distance a long and drawn out drive. I felt like a foreigner from not only another country, but also another time as I sat in the back seat of the private security firm's Mercedes mini van. In a country with unpredictable political unrest, the safety of Woodside personnel wasn't going to be taken for granted. A drive that should have taken only 15 minutes ended up taking 45 minutes, the traffic bumper-to-bumper and crawling at a snails pace.

After finally arriving at the Woodside Yangon office I was introduced to all the staff and advised that I could use the driver to do any sightseeing I wanted to do during the afternoon. I probably should have visited the famous Shwedagon Pagoda but after driving past a local fitness centre close to the Woodside office, I thought I would prefer to go for a workout to shake out the travel stiffness and also check out what the fitness industry in Yangon was like.

The driver took me to the hotel where I checked in and quickly changed into some workout gear and then jumped back into the waiting car and got dropped off at the gym. I made sure to take the special mobile phone with me so I could call the driver when I was ready to be picked up.

The gym was in a relatively new building and looked very modern compared to the surrounding buildings in the district. After checking in at the ground floor reception area I walked up the stairs to the second floor where the gym equipment was. The gym floor was very spacious with all new modern machines and free weights.

There were about six young local guys training when I arrived and I think they must never have seen a woman doing chin-ups before because after doing a few warm-up sets on the chin-up bar they started treating me like a celebrity and wanted to have photos taken with me. They all spoke English and were fun to talk to and we joked around for the rest of my workout. It was a nice way to spend my first day in Myanmar and I felt right at home in the gym, talking about training with the enthusiastic young guys.

With the workout finished I headed downstairs and was relieved to see the driver waiting for me, sparing me the hassle of having to work out how to use a phone that doesn't have a touch screen.

The Yangon Novatel hotel was very comfortable and actually had the most amazing gym I've ever seen in a hotel. It had better equipment than the public gym I had just trained in, but I was grateful for the gym session with the locals and didn't regret spending the money on it. Matching the impressive gym was an equally impressive health spa. With the prospect of spending the next 3 to 4 weeks working 12 hours a day on the rig I thought I might as well spoil myself with a massage while I had the chance.

The driver was waiting for me outside the reception area downstairs when I arrived early the next morning to check out. Being early in the morning meant the traffic wasn't quite as bad as it had been the afternoon before, so it only took 15 minutes to get to the airport.

The helicopter check-in area was downstairs in the domestic terminal and we were then taken to a room upstairs where we viewed the helicopter briefing video. We were led outside to an awaiting bus that drove us along the tarmac to the helicopter that was being prepared for departure.

The flight out to the rig took about an hour, with over half of that time spent flying over land. Once we cleared the built-up area of Yangon we were flying over mostly agricultural land, with frequent sightings of gold-roofed pagodas scattered throughout the countryside.

As we came into our approach on the Deepwater Millennium it felt like I'd never left home – we could still have been offshore from Western Australia for all I knew. Once you get back on the rig it doesn't matter where in the world you are because it's still all the same faces, same rooms and same routine, wherever in the world the well is being drilled. It's just a big floating office that picks up and moves around the world from one well to the next. No matter where it is, at the end of your hitch a helicopter will be there to pick you up and start your journey back home – wherever in the world that may be. There really isn't any other job like working on an offshore oilrig.

Once onboard, it was back to work and catching up on what stage the drilling was at. After a long break it's always fun catching up with everyone again and getting back into the day-to-day routine offshore. At least half of the 180 people on board were people who had been on the Woodside drilling campaign for as long as I had been on it, with the other half being short-term National personnel from local areas. There was now a Burmese-speaking interpreter onboard who translated all the PA announcements and safety meetings.

The standard of the meals had dropped since the rig left Australia, but as long as I didn't have to do any cooking or cleaning I was happy to live on boiled eggs, bananas and oranges if I had to, although bananas and oranges were pretty scarce within a few days of groceries being delivered so it was always nice when the containers of fresh food arrived on the decks.

Within 24 hours of being on the rig I was back into a routine of going to the gym, having breakfast then working from 6am to 6pm every day. The drilling was very unpredictable given the lack of previous drilling in the area, so we had to be prepared for any eventualities. We were virtually entering unknown territory in the deeper formations we drilled through so the operations were being monitored very closely by the Woodside operations personnel in Perth via the real-time data feed.

Shwe Yee Htun-1 intersected net gas pay as interpreted within the primary target interval and wireline evaluation of the prospect provided evidence of a working petroleum system in the deep water zone of the Rakhine Basin. This discovery was an encouraging outcome for future exploration and appraisal activity in the area as it de-risked some of the unknown leads within the field.

Although this would be my last hitch on the Deepwater Millennium, the drillship would continue to drill another well, Thalin-1, in the northern part of the Rakhine Basin approximately 60 km west of the Daewoo-operated producing Shwe Field, which has onshore gas plant and pipeline gas export facilities. This well would also intersect a gas column within the primary target interval and successfully prove a working petroleum system and a new play type different to that encountered at Shwe Yee Htun-1. These discoveries provided evidence of the high quality of offshore Myanmar as an exploration focus area.

The two discoveries at opposite ends of the Rakhine Basin was a great result for Woodside and were very encouraging for future exploration and appraisal activity, given the significant footprint Woodside has in Myanmar.

With the wireline logging operations completed on Shwe Yee Htun-1, Mitch and I were again scheduled to depart the rig the next day. Several months earlier we had already been rostered to work on another rig after this well was completed so we knew this would be our last hitch on the Deepwater Millennium. With only one well remaining to be drilled in Myanmar, we weren't likely to be needed on it again.

I had now worked for over 3½ years on the two Transocean rigs, the Legend and the Deepwater Millennium, so it was a bit sad having to pack all of my gear for the last time and say goodbye to everyone. Before boarding the helicopter, I threw out all of my accommodation clothes and my coveralls that I'd worn every day for the past 2 years, and packed my boots and few personal items that had been stored in a locker in the ladies change room.

I had been lucky enough to be involved with two long-term drilling campaigns but that was coming to an end now and I'd just be working from one well to the next from now on. With the dramatic drop in the price of oil since July 2014, many of the rigs worldwide had been stacked as drilling programs dried up. The Millennium was to be no exception and the rig, and all of its crew, was facing being made redundant after drilling the next well in Myanmar. It was a tense time for everyone working on the rig, as we never knew if each hitch was going to be our last. With the chopping block slowly working its way through the workforce, any breach of the rules could mean you would be on the next chopper out of there – for good. If you got caught with your mobile phone out on the deck, you were gone; if you were caught smoking where you shouldn't have been – see ya later! Every day when the chopper took a crew home you knew many of those people wouldn't be coming back. And now I was one of those people.

Although my time on the rig in Myanmar was up, I wasn't quite ready to cut ties with the country. The week after I was to leave the rig, the Yangon Marathon was being held in the city. Once I knew for sure that I wouldn't be working that weekend, I applied for a Myanmar tourist visa, which could be done online. I was advised not to participate in the marathon on the current business visa that Woodside had supplied for me to be able to work in the country, so I had to fly all the way home to Australia and re-enter the country as a tourist and at my own expense. Which I did. After only being home for a few days I flew back to Yangon to run the marathon in January 2016.

This time when I arrived at the airport in Yangon there

was no one to greet me and no company car to drive me to the hotel. I felt very much like a tourist as I accepted a lift from a young local offering me a taxi ride to my hotel. Fortunately he spoke enough English so I could ask him to take me to the marathon exhibition first, so I could pick up my race number. I had the details of the expo on a printed sheet showing the location, which he was able to understand and was happy to take me there first before dropping me off at the hotel.

Once we arrived at the expo I asked the taxi driver if he could come in with me so he could find out the details of the race start time and location so he could drive me there the next morning. He wasn't too happy about picking me up at 4am on a Sunday morning to drive me to the start line the next day, but after we negotiated a generous fare to make it worth his while he gave in and agreed to get me to the start line on time. I was very nervous about whether he would show up but I had no choice but to take his word for it. Fortunately he was true to his word and got me there in plenty of time for the early start at 5am the next morning.

Once at the start location, I met up with veteran fellow "Marathon Globetrotters" Brent Weiner and Rich Holmes, who between them had run hundreds of marathons around the world. With the Yangon Marathon being my 35th marathon but only the 14th different country I had run a marathon in, I was a relative newcomer to the Marathon Globetrotters club. Myanmar would be the 99th country Brent had run a marathon in and the 74th country for Rich – unbelievable! We also met Marathon Globetrotters newcomer Chau Smith, from Singapore, who was working towards running a marathon in 10 different countries to become a full member of the Marathon Globetrotters Club.

During the race around the streets of Yangon, there was amazing crowd support from the locals and I soon realised that responding to their cheers and giving them a thumbs up got them really excited. I got the feeling they looked upon the foreign runners, as somewhat of celebrities and it made them feel good just receiving recognition from us. I'm sure my picture is on hundreds of iPhones in Yangon as everyone was taking photos as I ran past.

In the second half of the marathon the route had us running along the Inya Lake embankment and I got caught up in a wedding party who were having their photos taken along the edge of the lake. I'm not sure if I was gatecrashing their photo session or they were gate-crushing my marathon but either way, we had fun sharing the path.

Despite the heat and humidity (and the "funky" street smells) I managed to finish the marathon in 4 hrs 5 min, which was a Boston and New York City marathon qualifying time for me for 2017. I really enjoyed my time in Myanmar, both on and off the rig. Hopefully I'll get to return one day soon as the deep water exploration and appraisal drilling intensifies in the Rakhine Basin. It would be great to be involved with a long-term drilling campaign in Myanmar so I could get to spend more time in Yangon and maybe even get to visit Shwedagon Pagoda!

Chapter 24

2016

WOODSIDE
CARNARVON BASIN, WA

Six days after returning from Yangon, I flew to Perth for a well briefing at the Woodside office before flying out to the Atwood Eagle, which was preparing to drill two wells in the offshore Beagle sub-basin.

The Beagle sub-basin is located in the Northern Carnarvon Basin. The two planned wells to be drilled were required to meet permit work plan commitments in the offshore exploration blocks. The rig location was approximately 65 km north east of Dampier and in 60 metres of water. This was a big change after the nearly

301

2,000 metres water depth of the last well I was on in Myanmar.

The Atwood Eagle is a column stabilized semi-submersible drilling unit that was constructed in 1982 and later upgraded in 2002. Being so long since its upgrade, it was now looking very old and tired. There was bed space for 120 people but the cabins were mostly 4-man rooms with a bathroom shared between two rooms, which meant eight men shared each bathroom. There was one 4-man cabin reserved for women so there could never be more than four women on the rig at any one time. The day I was to fly on there were two other women on board so I would be sharing the room with them.

The Eagle was much smaller in size than any other rig I'd been on so it was easy to find my way around it when I first arrived. After finishing the rig induction I headed to the mudlogging unit and started preparing for the drilling to start. Throughout that day there was word of a possible cyclone forming north of where the rig was situated so everyone was waiting to hear if there would be a cyclone evacuation in the coming days.

When I left the logging unit to go to bed at about 8pm there was still no definite decision made on whether they would start an evacuation the next day but it was looking highly likely they would be. I went to bed knowing that I could be on a chopper the very next morning and heading home again.

I was sleeping on the top bunk bed in the cabin and woke early so I could go to the gym before starting work. Not being used to the ladder on the bed, I leant my weight backwards as I reached for the railing around the end of the bed but didn't realise the curtain was over it and my hand was unable to grab hold of the rail. Unfortunately, in my half-asleep state, I had already committed my body weight backwards down over the ladder and when my hand failed to grab hold of the railing I started an uncontrolled decent from the top bunk, crashing flat on my back onto the narrow patch of floor between the two bunks. The lady in the other top bunk bed sprung up and asked if I was OK as my crashing body-slam echoed through the room. Surprisingly my head managed to miss all the other obstacles in the narrow space between the beds and after laying still for a few moments while I checked that my back was still in one piece and operational, I slowly got to my feet. I was definitely awake now!

After letting my room mate know I was OK, she informed me that I would be on the first chopper that morning as they started preparing for a cyclone evacuation. I was definitely not off to a good start on this rig and could only hope that things would improve. After packing up all the work documents that I'd unpacked in the mudlogging unit only the day before, I was on the chopper bound for Karratha, Perth and eventually back home that same night and sleeping in my own bed. That was the shortest hitch offshore I'd ever done.

I had 17 days at home before finally being called back to work on the Eagle. By the time I got out there, Mitch was already on board and overseeing the drilling of the top-hole section. The other women who had been on the rig the first time I was there had now gone so for the next few days I would have the room to myself. It gave me a chance to grab a bottom bunk before anyone else came into the room.

The one redeeming feature about the Eagle was its food. The Atwood Oceanics rigs were well known for their great food as they used their own cooks, rather than a third party catering company like many other rigs. Not only were all the main meals amazing but they also had a night pastry cook who baked fresh bread every night and also amazing cakes and other pastries. Dave, the pastry cook, was also a legendary marathon runner who clocked sub-elite finishing times for the 42 km event in his veteran category. I was a slow plodder compared to him.

The galley even had a NutriBullet that the crew could use so I was able to make myself a banana smoothie after my training session each morning. There was always plenty of fresh fruit and avocados and all the things I would normally eat at home that I'd never see when I was working offshore. By the end of my first week on the rig the galley staff were already welcoming me with a raw egg for my banana smoothie as soon as I walked into the galley for breakfast. It's often the small things that make a big difference when you're working away from home.

Unfortunately, there were lots of bad parts to this hitch, which the great food had trouble making up for. Just before I had flown back onto the rig the air-conditioners in the gym had broken down and it would take at least two weeks to get replacements brought in. Now that wouldn't normally be too much of a concern except for the fact that the gym was a metal shipping container that sat out on the deck in the tropical sun, heat and humidity all day – and it had no windows that you could open. Fortunately I trained at 3 –

4am in the morning so it was at its coolest at that time of the day, but it was still unbelievably hot and humid in there. The floor was usually wet from the condensed humidity and for the people who would have been training after work hours at 7pm it would have been like a sauna in there. I was always glad to get up on the helideck for a cool-down walk after my workout.

The last week of the hitch also saw the air-conditioners in the mudlogging unit breakdown, and like the gym, it is a metal shipping container that sits out on the open deck in the sun all day, and it's also full of computer equipment that generated even more heat. With seven people working out of the small container it was very difficult for everyone to "keep their cool" while we waited for a technician to fly out to repair it.

Given the current depressed state of the oil and gas industry, the morale on the rig was at an all-time low with everyone concerned about their future after the end of these two wells. A "Stand Down For Safety" meeting was called on day shift one day to address the morale issue and to re-enforce the need for everyone to remain focussed on the job. The message of how bad things were was harped on throughout the meeting so if you weren't already depressed about the work situation before the meeting then you definitely were by the time you walked out of the meeting. For most people, this could be their last hitch of work for the foreseeable future so it was hard for people not to be concerned about their job security. Working offshore was all many of these people knew so the prospect of not being able to do it any longer was starting to hit home.

While Woodside still had drilling they planned to do, it wasn't clear what rigs they would use to do it. The plan kept changing from one month to the next and as stories of drilling campaigns being put on hold continued to be reported in the news, nothing could be guaranteed in the months to come.

With every rig that got "cold stacked" there were hundreds of workers being made redundant. It wasn't dependent on your experience or your position – it just came down to where you were when the music stopped.

With the Beagle sub-basin wells completed it was time to leave the Atwood Eagle and head back home to the Gold Coast. I didn't know how long it would be before I'd be back on a rig but hopefully not too long. Now it's my turn to play the waiting game.

EPILOGUE

Stopping work didn't mean I had to stop learning. I registered to attend a 5-day "Integrated Petrophysics for Reservoir Characterisation" course in Perth in May and prior to attending that, I completed the Boston Marathon, for the third time, in April.

With more time on my hands I've had a chance to reflect on how much I've achieved over the 30+ years of my career and how far I've come since I was that graduate geologist in Bendigo in 1983. I have packed up and moved the family home eleven times in those 30 years, never regretting any of those moves as we followed the work. Writing this book has made me realise I've worked too hard for too long to give up on the industry now. I don't intend to make Chapter 24 the final chapter of my offshore career.

May 2016 saw an increase in the International rig count for the first time in 18 months. Although it was only a modest increase it was still an increase, giving a glimmer of hope of better times to come. Busts are always eventually followed by boom times so you just have to be patient and wait for the cycle to continue on its path. But most importantly, make sure you're in the best possible position to jump on board when the industry rebounds.

Being single with no relationship commitments and having dependent adult children means my life is free to go in any direction I choose to take it, and able to take advantage of career opportunities as they arise. It's both exciting and scary not knowing what the future holds but I'm sure there are lots more adventures ahead of me yet, and more books to write.

There are still lots of countries I haven't worked in, or run marathons in, so the journey continues.

ABOUT THE AUTHOR

Amanda Barlow is a contract geologist who has worked within the minerals, coal seam gas and offshore oil and gas industries – a career spanning over 30 years. She is also a recreational marathon runner and a published author. She has run nearly 40 marathons in 15 different countries around the world, including the Jungle Marathon, in Brazil, the story of which was told in her first published book:

"Call of the Jungle – How a Camping-Hating City-Slicker Mum Survived an Ultra Endurance race through the Amazon Jungle" (available in print and kindle version on Amazon.com).

Follow "An Inconvenient Life" on Facebook at https://www.facebook.com/AnInconvenientLife

Made in the USA
Lexington, KY
31 October 2018